Thomas Sergeant Perry

From Opitz to Lessing

Thomas Sergeant Perry

From Opitz to Lessing

ISBN/EAN: 9783743373303

Manufactured in Europe, USA, Canada, Australia, Japa

Cover: Foto ©Thomas Meinert / pixelio.de

Manufactured and distributed by brebook publishing software (www.brebook.com)

Thomas Sergeant Perry

From Opitz to Lessing

FROM

OPITZ TO LESSING:

A STUDY OF PSEUDO-CLASSICISM IN LITERATURE.

BY

THOMAS SERGEANT PERRY,

AUTHOR OF "ENGLISH LITERATURE IN THE EIGHTEENTH CENTURY."

BOSTON:

JAMES R. OSGOOD AND COMPANY.

1885.

STEREOTYPED BY
C. J. PETERS & SON, BOSTON.

TO

W. D. HOWELLS.

PREFACE.

THE aim of this book is to give some
few of the many available proofs that the
different nations of modern Europe have
passed through very nearly the same experience in literature since the Renaissance.
The course of each separate nation has been
described by hosts of writers: in France
the early glow of the Pleiad, the chastening
correctness of Malherbe and Boileau, the
gradual romantic revival; in England, the
fading out of the Elizabethan fervour,
the precision of Dryden and Pope, and the
modifications that led to the revival of
poetry; the similar course of events in
Germany, — all these things have been set
forth in countless volumes. The facts once
established, it becomes possible to detect a
harmony which it would be rash to call co-
incidence. The next thing is obviously to

Chuquet 1926,

see how closely the various nations kept step together. Until this is done, our knowledge is fragmentary and incomplete; the relation of different authors to one another is often only intelligible when we see it more brilliantly illustrated in another country. After this work is finished, there will remain the task of ascertaining exactly to what extent each nation modified the general course of literary movement; what was the national equation, so to speak, of each country. When this is ascertained, the period treated will be really known; until then it will not be fully comprehended.

This volume is offered to the public as a slight essay to show how like were some of the early movements in different countries.

T. S. P.

Boston, July 28, 1884.

FROM OPITZ TO LESSING: `

A STUDY OF PSEUDO-CLASSICISM.

CHAPTER I.

WHAT we include in the term "German Literature" may be conveniently assumed to have begun with Lessing ; but, in order to understand what that eminent writer did in the way of clearing the ground for his successors and of laying the foundations on which they were to work, it is important to take a look backwards, and to see what had been done and what left undone before his day. Only in this way can we appreciate him at his proper value, and an examination of this sort may also be of service, by showing us that the study of literature, which is, after all, only the study of one part of history, is fruitful even when it requires of us that we give our attention to men of moderate merit, to writers who are praised when they are called second-rate. There is something fascinating in studying merely the greatest men, and in passing over the rest without thought ; but literature cannot be understood in that way, any more than botany can be learned by studying nothing but Japanese lilies and Jacqueminot roses, or modern history by giving all our attention to Napoleon Bonaparte, Washington, and Lincoln. In literature, the man who accomplishes anything great is the one man who succeeds where countless others fail ; and our study will be of little profit if it does not teach us how much greater are the long and silently prepared movements than any brilliant performance, how the most striking thing about any genius is its inevitableness, and that it cannot be understood without the comprehension of the whole spirit of the time. It is to the Germans that we owe

the statement of this principle, and it is only
just to illustrate its truth by investigating
what their writers have contributed to the
world's delight.   We shall see, then, that
literature is not something remote from
human interest, although the way in which
it is often studied and sometimes practised
may encourage this unsound view.   Let us
begin with the principle that literature is
not a thing apart from life, but is humanity
recording its hopes, thoughts, fears, and
emotions, not humanity composing rhetorical exercises, except, to be sure, at moments
when rhetorical exercises are the legitimate
expression of corrupt taste and artificial enthusiasms; and even these, when viewed in
this way, acquire new interest in our eyes.

Although the modern literature of Germany begins only in the latter half of the
last century, there had been a time when
Germany was in the van.   Even if the
minnesingers were second to the Provençal
troubadours, they were second to them

alone. Later, when England was without commerce or manufactures, before the age of Elizabeth, Germany was a rich and powerful country. At the beginning of the sixteenth century the German artists were the only rivals of the Italian. The Reformation, which was the second great modern movement, was the work of Germany alone. Learning, art, progress, wealth, flourished in that great country. How was it that these things were lost? How did it happen that this mighty country was shattered into a host of petty and powerless provinces, without distinctive trait or perceptible influence, for something like two hundred years? While England stepped forth in the age of Elizabeth to the position of the great Protestant country, with a literature that has been rivalled only by Greece in its brief flowering time ; and Spain won dominion over half of Europe; and France became the lawgiver in literature, politics, philosophy, and fashions, to all civilized nations; and even Holland, the meagre little country, defeated the Spaniards and founded something like a world-empire, — Germany sank from its high place into a mere incoherent mass of principalities. Its work seemed forever closed. So true is this, that there seems a chasm between the Germany of the Reformation and the Germany of the last century, and a chasm which had swallowed wealth, art, literature — in a word, every sign of prosperity. The history of the decadence of Germany is most painful reading. The briefest possible summary of it will show the gradual steps of material and intellectual decline. There is no need of fearing that a description of it does not belong to literary history. It is only by refreshing our knowledge of these facts that we can understand why a blight fell upon letters and arts for so long a time, and by what measures the greater man who followed attempted to undo its mischievous effects. We know from our own experience that our own study or thought is affected by all sorts of external incidents. If there is some one ill in the next room, or if the town is full of excitement, our work is interrupted, and what is true of every person is obviously true of all persons. It is only by knowing these external conditions that we can begin to comprehend what the German writers said and did.

In the first place, the Reformation tore the country into two bleeding factions. The Church of Rome was far too powerful to yield its supremacy without a bitter struggle in which freedom of conscience was met by another strong principle, the sense of obedience, a feeling that had so long been nurtured that it had acquired enormous power. Moreover, the Reformation was, in a great measure, the result of the new spirit of the Renaissance, — a spirit which had grown in Germany more than elsewhere, because, before the discovery of America, Germany had been one of the main avenues by which the modern spirit made its way from Italy to the rest of Europe. But when America was discovered, the Mediterranean lost its central position, and the Atlantic Ocean at once became the new and larger field for maritime enterprise. It was a change that affected the great Hanseatic cities of Germany in exactly the same way as the opening of the vast wheat fields of the West has affected the agriculture of New England. Communication with India, which before this had been made through Alexandria and Venice into Germany, now followed the longer but more profitable voyage around the Cape of Good Hope, thus robbing Germany of its previous share of a most profitable trade. We see at once the centre of power abandoning Germany and moving to the west of Europe. Holland, England, Portugal, France, and Spain, secured what Germany lost, and that unhappy country was left to carry on a most momentous struggle with swiftly dwindling forces. With the decay of the material importance of the country came what we have all seen, on an infinitely smaller scale, in New England towns and villages that once were prosperous, and, in their prosperity, full of energy, and now are lifeless accumulations of empty houses and shiftless citizens.

Then in Germany came the Thirty Years' War (1618–48). This was a terrible blow to the country. We may well doubt whether in the whole history of modern times there is a chapter of such hopeless gloom and terrible tragedy. Let us bear in mind, however, that it must not receive all the blame for the decay of Germany; it has enough to endure without that. The deterioration had begun before hostilities broke out. War is not always merely destruction ; not always are the bravest slain without good to the country and to the world. We ourselves know that even out of civil war there may rise a grander comprehension of patriotism, fuller material growth, a broader view of a nation's duties and responsibilities; but the Thirty Years' War was like a plague or an earthquake. The prosperity of the country received a blow from which it did not recover for over two centuries. A few statistics will make this clear. In Würtemberg the population was reduced from 400,000 to 48,000; in Frankenthal, from 18,000 to 324. Elsewhere more than half the houses, and more than two thirds of the inhabitants, had perished; in yet another place but one tenth of the population survived. In Berlin there were left only three hundred citizens. And these figures make no account of the horrors of the conflict for the living. A flame of anarchy had passed over the whole country, and consumed all feeling of security and mutual dependence. The country was left in ruins, and moral confidence was almost wholly gone. To be sure, the leaders made what seemed to them their profit out of the general confusion; but the use they made of it, as we shall soon see, was of a most unfortunate kind.

Already, at the time of the Reformation, the theologians had confounded the intellectual zeal of the Renaissance with the perils coming from the Roman church, and denounced them both with bitterness. The Humanists were looked upon as public enemies. The universities had shut their doors to new truths and clung obstinately to the old scholasticism. The Renaissance had been rather a theological movement than one of literary and artistic fervor, as it was in other countries, although Hans Sachs, Dürer, and Cranach showed that the tide was turning in this direction, in spite of the more exclusively theologic bent which Luther gave to it. But this advance was of course lost in the Thirty Years' War. When the country at last found peace, a new generation had grown up that had known nothing but turmoil, and the work of civilization had almost to begin anew at a remote point. The rulers and the nobility had wholly lost touch with their own country and begun to model themselves after the French, who then, under Louis XIII. and XIV., were imposing their standard of taste on all Europe, and this change is one that requires our closest attention.

We must remember that the Gallomania which henceforth prevailed in Germany cannot be explained simply as the result of more intimate acquaintance with the French who had taken part in the war; nor was it by any means peculiar to Germany alone. To be sure, it struck deeper there than elsewhere. Every princeling maintained his court like a miniature Versailles; he generally constructed a little fortress which was garrisoned by a handful of soldiers, who were drilled like the mighty armies of France. Germany was spotted over with these reduced copies of

its great neighbor, when every vice and extravagance that were destroying the foundations of a mighty kingdom were keeping
the impoverished Germans in misery. Augustus the Strong, of Saxony, spent, on a
single festival, an amount that is variously
estimated as from one to five millions of
thalers; on another, about four millions.
Karl Eugene, of Würtemberg, maintained a
suite of two thousand persons. Augustus
the Strong had set five hundred peasants
and two hundred and fifty miners to work
destroying a forest in order to make a
pleasure-ground. Their more serious em-
ployments and interests may be gathered
from the mention of a struggle which agi-
tated the princely houses who envied the
privilege that the electoral (*kurfürstliche*)
ambassadors enjoyed of having their chairs
on the same carpet as the Imperial Chief
Commissioner. Finally, their princely
hearts glowed with manly pride when di-
plomacy decided that their ambassadors

might sit with the two front legs of their chairs on the fringes of the carpet.

The whole country swarmed with officials. Positions were bought; professorships were sometimes the property of minors. The two thousand principalities into which Germany was divided, suffered, although not equally, from these miseries. As Biedermann has pointed out, the whole population was divided into two classes — the official class and their victims. Everyone tried to become an official, and if he could do that, his interest led him to keep the others down. The full particulars of this condition of affairs cannot be given here, but it will be readily seen that the country was in a wretched state. We shall come across countless instances of the way in which this spirit manifested itself in literature, and we shall notice how great is its divergence from that of the early humanism. Yet this divergence is to be noticed in every country of Europe. In England the first inspiriting effect of the Renaissance flourished for some time in the magnificence of the Elizabethan drama. It finally succumbed before the courtly, artificial style which was prominent in the work of the early Italians, and in France won a speedy victory over the confused efforts of Hardy, and even over Corneille's early attempts to withstand the movement of the time in the direction of classicism, and away from the union of mediævalism with classicism, that began so well in England. In Germany, as is well known, the beginning had been very promising. Hans Sachs struck a note which showed clearly that the new influence was combining with the old one, and it would have been natural to expect that literature in Germany would have flourished, for a time at least, with an original fervour as characteristic as that of England and Spain before they succumbed to classicism. Yet, while those two countries gained new strength from their augmented material prosperity, Germany lost hers; and after the Thirty Years' War the coherent life of the country, already in decay, was destroyed. The shattered relations of the past could no more be resumed than a Shakespearian play can be written to-day in Boston, or than roses can bloom in snow and ice. The new tendency of civilization had begun the work of ruin, and the war completed the task.

Let us see if we may not find out some of the reasons for this momentous change, and our task will be the more interesting if we bear in mind that it was one which affected English literature as well as the German; though, for reasons to be pointed out, not to the same extent. It was a universal modification of enthusiasm in the direction of formal correctness. The sole model was Latin literature, and it is only apparent on examination how much the work of the old Roman writers has become an inspiration to modern civiliza-

tion.   In spite of the most ardent efforts
to extirpate mediævalism, its historic position could not be destroyed, although it
was much modified.   Yet the natural
consequence of copying the literature of
another race,— written, too, in a language
that was swiftly becoming a dead one,—
was this: that literature fell entirely into
the hands of the learned, and became an
aristocratic possession.   And herein, too, it
followed one of the strongest movements
of the time; indeed, it is fairer to say they
were both expressions of one thing,— the
predominance of aristocracy in every
department of thought, in government as
in odes, in the church as in education.

Let us bear in mind that, two centuries
ago, not only was the work of the ancients
the most admired model that the world
knew, but that there was then only beginning the momentous change — by no
means even now wholly accomplished —
which has modified the intellectual pro-

cesses of men as completely as steam has
modified their material condition. Just as
until within about half a century all travel-
ling was done by sail or with the aid of
horses, — in the time of Solomon and of
the Romans, as during our Revolutionary
War, — so, until the diffusion of the Coper-
nican system, men regarded their position
in the universe as the central one; the sun,
moon, and stars were thought to have
been created for their sole good; and it
also remained one of the accepted commonplaces of belief that men were the degenerate descendants of a more glorious race
of the past. Modern science has shown
the inaccuracy of this notion, and by so
doing has weakened our dependence on
classical literature. *Weakened*, I say, not
destroyed, for we cannot understand the
work of our ancestors without understanding what it was that they felt and endeavored to convey, and how it was
that they thought and wrote as they did.

But this historical interest, important though it be, is very different from dependence on the classics as the sole repository of profane learning, which was one important result of the Renaissance. The value of native literature is something that has only recently been learned, and it will be interesting to watch the steps by which this was done in Germany. After the Thirty Years' War, literature languished. The natural growth of the Renaissance had already begun to fail under the theological controversies that preceded that terrible tragedy. One of the most important of the efforts to atone for absence of inspiration by zealous work was the foundation of the Fruit-bearing Society in 1617, which was established for the purpose of encouraging literature. The inspiring model of this, and the similar societies that followed it, was the Italian Academies. The French Academy, which was founded in 1629, was another proof of the existence of similar needs in that country. Both the Academy and its humble rival, the Fruit-bearing Society, were intended as literary tribunals, which should find a way out of the confusion that darkened intellectual progress. The German society was composed of seven hundred and fifty members, among whom were authors, grammarians, philologists, rhetoricians, and a host of non-producers who were interested in literature. These were almost entirely people of gentle birth. The members were busily employed, according to their light, in polishing the language and introducing those graces of expression and manners which we shall soon see outwardly prominent in most of the modern nations. The war, however, interfered with this society; yet more fatal to it was the remoteness of its interests from the national life. While with one hand it turned towards the brilliant literatures of Italy and France and began to translate

the works that had won fame there, it
also kept on good terms with mediævalism, as was shown by Neumark's assertion
that Japhet's grandson had settled in As-
cania, — *i. e.*, the Duchy of Anhalt,— and
that among his direct descendants were
Manus, the first King of Germany, a contemporary of Abraham,[1] and the founder
of Trier; Servus, King of the Suabians,
etc., a genealogy which was demanded
by the alleged descent of the French from
Francus, the son of Hector, and of the
Britains from Brutus, a grandson of
Æneas.[2] It will be observed that the
Germans made up for their late arrival in
this fabulous antiquity by going back to a
remoter origin than other nations. Mat-

[1] Yet even in the new edition of the "Encyclopædia
Britannica," we read that "the Chinese Shoo-King" (the
Book of History) "takes us back to about the time of
Noah." — See vol. v., p. 660.

[2] For further mention of these genealogies see the very
interesting book of Arturo Graf, "Roma nella memoria
o nelle Immaginazione del Medio Evo." Turin, 1883:
i. 28, and note p. 53.

ters of orthography and spelling were de-
bated with much fervour. In general,
however, literature derived but little profit
from these well-meant endeavors to adapt
the country to the new light that was
rising. The lamentable divisions of the
country stood in the way of the formation
of any general enthusiasm, and each petty
principality was an intrenched camp where
lurked prejudice and ignorance.

When we learn that among the questions
discussed by the members of the society
was whether the Germans had any share in
building the Tower of Babel, and whether
the German language was spoken at Greece
and Rome, we are reminded of the subjects
given out by the French Academy for discussion just before the Revolution: " How
often was the Temple of Janus closed ? "
" What were the attributes of Jupiter Am-
mon? " etc., and we begin to doubt the
efficiency of academies in conveying enlightenment. Certainly the German society

scarcely verified its name. Its rivals were scarcely more fortunate. Some of them represented a violent reaction against French influence, but the subtler consequences of the new spirit manifested itself even in them. They sought to remove all Gallicisms from their language, but they could not keep from falling into line with the more important part of the movement, which represented to them, as to everyone, the advance of modern thought. It is sufficiently clear that they moved further and further away from any connection with popular literature, and herein they followed in the same direction with what was done in all the other countries of Europe. Yet nowhere was the discord more marked than in Germany. The explanation is in part that remote and foreign ideals were chosen from antiquity, but we must also remember that the schism was not caused by this fact alone. While the upper classes rose in education and what was in many ways refinement, the lower classes sank from the level of ease which they had enjoyed during the middle ages. They lost power, which was speedily grasped by the aristocracy. This was true throughout Europe, but nowhere was it truer than in Germany, where religious discussions and civil war had done their worst, and where arrogance on one side was met by servility on the other. The political history explains the literary, just as literature always illustrates the political, history of a country.

What, then, the societies which I have briefly mentioned actually accomplished, was slight. Altogether they did less than a single writer, Opitz, who was himself a member of the Fruit-bearing Society. They served to foster a general uniformity of taste; but the law, so to speak, was first laid down by Opitz. It was not a new law by any manner of means. Few laws are, for that matter. They are but the condensation of a widespread feeling, the statement

of a general desire. The modifications that
Opitz helped to introduce into Germany
were generally described as resulting from
French influence, and their sway in Germany was doubtless much furthered by the
predominance of French taste in this country as elsewhere, though this was more
marked in Germany than anywhere. Yet,
although the same tendency manifested
itself first with great distinctness, and was
followed in England by Ben Jonson, without knowledge of what was done in France,
the French acquired the completest mastery
of it, and gave it their name by right of
conquest, because they adapted and applied
it most successfully. It harmonized, too,
with the political system of which Louis
XIV. was the most eminent exponent, under whose hands France became a grand
and powerful country, while the German
imitations were ludicrous miniatures of its
splendor, just as their so-called Gallic literature was a mere confused echo of the
great French classic literature.

Opitz's *Buch von der deutschen Poeterei* was written and published in 1624. There is much in it that has a remote sound to our ears, but it had at the time all the charm of eternal truth. Here are some of its precepts:—

"Heroic verse excludes what is not suitable, and brings in much that does belong there, but is new and unexpected, introducing all sorts of fables, histories, arts of war, slaughters, councils, storms of wind, rain, and thunder, and whatever necessarily awakens our awe; and everything in such order as if one thing followed the other and came unsought into the book."

"Tragedy is suited for the majesty of heroic verse, except that it seldom permits the introduction of people of humble birth or common deeds, because it concerns itself with one of royal lineage, murders, despairs, slaughters of fathers and children, fires, incest, wars and tumults, lamentations, outcries, sighs, and such things."

"Comedy has to do with common matters and persons: it treats of weddings, banquets, games, the deceits and knaveries of servingmen, braggart foot-soldiers, love-matters, the frivolity of youth, the avarice of the aged, low amours, and such things which are daily occurrence among common people. Hence those who have nowadays written comedies have greatly erred, in that they have brought into them emperors and potentates, thereby running full in the face of the laws of comedy."

"Eclogues or pastoral songs have to do with sheep, goats, seagoing, harvests, fruits, fishing, and other outdoor things; and whatever the subject,— as love, marriages, deaths, courtships, banqueting, etc.,— it is treated in a rustic and simple manner."

"In elegies one finds first only sad things, but, afterwards, love matters, complaints about one's mistress, longing for death, letters, yearnings for the absent, narrations of one's life," etc.

This congeries of definitions and precepts was taken for the most part from the "Poetices" of J. C. Scaliger (1561), a book that first froze into solid shape the mass of pedantry that had grown up from the reading of the classics. In accordance with his principles, Opitz at once set himself to the work of translating abundantly the masterpieces of modern and ancient literature into German, a task which occupied all his contemporaries throughout Europe; and his real intellectual contemporaries, it is to be remembered, were the Pleiad among the French, and the early Elizabethans among the English. Thus he translated a play of Seneca's and the "Antigone" of Sophocles, a task which was part of the literary education of every country of Europe, as truly as it is part of the discipline of every well-educated young man. Thus, Dolce and others in Italy, the elder Baïf in France, and Gascoigne in England, to give but a few names, all began in the same way. Like Surrey, Opitz translated from the Italians, like Spenser, from the work of the French Pleiad; then he made use of the work of the Dutch writers, and notably of Heinsius, to say nothing of abundant versions of Greek, Latin, French, and Spanish writers. He put into German Barclay's "Argenis" and Sir Philip Sidney's "Arcadia." It was with these crutches that his best work was done. As an original writer he accomplished but little, — in this respect he may be compared with Malherbe, — but his influence was enormous. Other writers, and notably Paul Fleming, were endowed with greater poetical genius; but none of them said just what their contemporaries wanted to hear so infallibly as did Opitz, and hence his position was secure.

While under Opitz's directions, Germany took that step in her literary progress which was made by every country in Europe, and the new formal knowledge of the classics became the main foundation, instead of being one of many elements, of literature. There were other modifications, here as elsewhere, which it is proper for us to observe distinctly. The new interest in the classics was the main change, the others are distinctly secondary varieties of this one great substitution of the history, mythology, manner of thought of Rome, and of Greece as seen by the Romans, in the place of the natural past of each nation. In everything done in art and literature for two centuries, we perceive a new background. The old ideals are wiped out and scraps of classical antiquity are brought in to take their place.

To be sure, throughout the middle ages, Roman literature had served this purpose, but now it was burnished anew and had its missing limbs restored. Moreover, it held alone the position that it had previously shared — as in Chaucer's Canterbury Tales — with purely mediæval legends. When Opitz said that it was of the highest importance to make a proper selection of epithets, of which previously there had been a great lack, and that they were to be gathered especially from Greek and Latin, he foretold the course which writers were to follow for a long time. When he illustrated his meaning by examples taken from Latin writers, he used the only models that were authoritative. When he advised the employment of full and forcible phrases in speaking of important subjects, as gods, heroes, princes, cities, etc., and that these should not be simply named but described with high and splendid language, citing Vergil's method as an example; — when he did this, I say, he won the glory which falls to that rare man who gives advice that is followed. Possibly this is not always the best advice; but, however this may be, we must remember that it is not Opitz who spoke; he was but the mouthpiece of the new spirit. The authority of the classics, which was thus asserting itself, was simply the authority of the best that men had uttered on the problems of life and, what is perhaps the most important, of the best way of uttering it; for it was a rhetorical change almost as much as anything else.

CHAPTER II.

In studying the pseudo-classicism we notice three distinct steps that it took,— three currents of the movements of the Renaissance. The first in time was that which we have just seen in our brief examination of Opitz; and Opitz personifies the whole movement in German literature, for it is always convenient, in dealing with the past, to condense a great deal into one proper name. Thus, Leonidas stands for the Greek resistance to Persia; Washington, for the whole course of our revolutionary war; Pope, for the classical wave in English literature. The second one, which also took its rise in Italy, was a form of writing of which elegance and conceits were the most admired constituents. It was a refinement of the rugged virtues of

31

the school of Trissino and Rucellai in Italy; of that of Ronsard, even Malherbe, and the earlier Jodelle in France, and of Ben Jonson in England. In England it formed what we know as the metaphysical school of poetry. The third was the French classicism which began in England with Dryden and flourished under Pope, and pervaded Germany under the hands of Canitz and Gottsched. It is the second one that we have now to examine; and while it is part of the advantage to be got from studying a foreign literature, that it throws light upon our own, our own in its turn also throws light upon that of its neighbors. Hence it is quite possible for us to follow the further vagaries of German literature by studying the corresponding excuses in the English poets. What we shall notice will be a similar loosening of the hold upon simplicity, and the search for exaggerated refinement in both. This is soon conspicuous in the works of Klaj

(1616–1656) and of Harsdörffer (1607–
1658), for the German side, who may be
compared with some of their English contemporaries; and, indeed, the simultaneous
study of what was done in the two countries will be of service in showing how
inevitable are what every writer takes to
be his best claims to originality. We hum-
bler people might as well be proud of the
fact that we shiver when we are cold, or
put on airs of superiority because we
strictly follow fashion in dress.

Let us, in the first place, notice that the
delicate observation of the beauty of flowers, trees, and gardens is common to the
corresponding poets in the two languages.
In his "Blumenlied" Harsdörffer sings: —

> Die Blümelein sind ohne Zahl,
> und geben uns die freye Wahl,
> die schönsten auszulesen.
> Von Ost und Westen schaut man hier
> die wunder seltne Blumen-zier,
> so jemals sind gewesen.
> Der Safft, hat Krafft

und das Leben, eingegeben,
der sie mahlet,
ja mit Purpur-Blut bestralet.
Es bleibet bey der Blumen nicht,
die Bäumen bringen ihr Gericht,
die Pfirsing und Marilen :
Die Weichsel, Feigen, und Granat
und was man in der Fremde, hat,
kan man hierum erzielen
Citron, Melon, etc.

Observe, too, " Das Vogelsang " : —

Nachtigal führe der Vögelein Reyen !
Töne, wann andre freyen in Maien,
Lispele, wispel Reuter zum Pferd,
klage mit schlagen, mache dich wehrt !
Lasse das zarte Stimmelein steigen
Orgel und Pfeiffen, Lauten und Geigen,
müssen verstummend gegen dir schweigen.

Read, too, Philipp von Zesen's "An seine Gedanken bei herzunahendem Frühlinge," as well as numberless other poems of the time, and there is to be found, in colder language, the same innocent delight in nature that is conspicuous in Herrick (1591–1674?), and Marvell (1620–1678), to mention the most conspicuous. Indeed, the more we examine, the more striking becomes the likeness; we seem to be reading duller Herricks, and Marvells, and Carews, and Herberts. What shall we examine first? The mere form of the poems? We may recall, to take the most singular examples, Herbert's poems, "The Altar," in which the lines, by being longer at the beginning and at the end, with all the intervening ones of uniformly smaller size, give to the eye a crude representation of an altar; his "Easter Wings," in which we notice a similar process of imitation; and Herrick's "Pillar of Fame." This ingenious device, which was known in Greece, practised in the East, and was a favorite form in the Middle Ages, found many admirers in Germany at about the same time. Similarly constructed poems still survive, it is curious to notice, in valentines, a form of composition in which one is safe in not expecting originality. In these conventional productions we find, as we should

expect, relics of a distant past. Not every
one writes valentines every year, and those
who do, adopt a form that has, at the most,
one three hundred and sixty-fifth as much
wear as the more usual forms of correspon-
dence. Hence, methods are preserved that
attrition has rendered obsolete elsewhere.
Indeed, the very gew-gaws of the paper on
which valentines are printed have kept
alive old forms of decoration contemporary
with the lyric inspiration that endears them
to the receiver, just as the oldest fashions
are preserved in court and ecclesiastical
dresses, — especially of higher dignitaries,
— and in the unfrequent ceremony of
coronation. In time, perhaps, it may be
possible to make a chronological table of
these curious survivals, of cross-bows as
well as valentines, and to estimate the date
when they flourished by the age of those
who now make use of them.

Harsdörffer composed an "Abbildung
des Reichsapfels" and an "Abbildung des

zweispitzigen Parnassus." [1]   Another curious form is exemplified in Herrick's "Upon Love, by way of Question and Answer:" —

> I bring ye love? *Quest.*— What will love do?
> *Ans.*— Like, and dislike ye.
> I bring ye love. *Quest.*— What will love do?
> *Ans.*— Stroke ye, to strike ye.
> I bring ye love. *Quest.*— What will love do?
> *Ans.*— Love will befool ye, *etc.*

With this curious form, which is doubtless an inheritance from the Middle Ages, we may compare Hellwig's "Wechselgesang:" —

> *Helianthus* — Es klappern, und plappern, und pappern,
> *Montano* — in Nesten die Störche.
>   Es tirililiret, tiliret, umschwüret,
> *Hel.*— in Lüften die Lerche.
>   Es kittert, und flittert, sich wittert,
> *Mont.*— der Stiglitz bey Tag.
>   Es zwitzert, und witzert, und zizert
> *Hel.* — das Zeisslein in Haag.

[1] The student will recall many further illustrations of what is but mentioned here,— *e.g.*, the prefatory lines to Sylvester's "Du Bartas," and Schottelius's "Pocal von Dactilischen und Anapestischen."

Herrick's "Aphorisms" and Logau's "Sinngedichte" correspond equally. As for the more intimate similarities of thought, the resemblances are even more striking. Scheffler's poem comparing Jesulein to a Blümelein,—

> Ich weiss ein liebes Blümelein
> Mit Gottes Thau begossen,
> In einem jungfräulichen Schrein
> Zur Winters-zeit entsprossen:
> Diss Blümelein heisst Jesulein,
> Ew'ger Jugend, grosser Tugend,
> Schön und lieblich, reich und herrlich:
> Menschen-kind,
> Wie selig ist, der dieses Blümelein findt.

is a good example of what in England expressed itself in poems like Herbert's "Jesu," where we find the same quality of conceit, although in another guise than here. The spirit that animates the "Vanitas! Vanitatum Vanitas!" of Gryphius is the same that we find in Herbert's "Home:"

> Nothing but drought and dearth, but bush and brake,
> Which way so e'er I look, I see;

Some may dream merrily, but when they wake,
They dress themselves, and come to Thee.

. . . .

We talk of harvests — there are no such things
But when we leave our corn and hay;
There is no fruitful yeare but that which brings
The last and lov'd, though dreadful day.

When we come to Hofman von Hofmanswaldau (1618–1679) we reach a man
who gave extreme expression to those vagaries that are conspicuous in what are
called the metaphysical poets of England,
from Donne to Cowley. But, before we
take up these grotesque excesses, we may
note how in the lines " An Doris " he uses
the same similes and preaches the same
lesson that we find in Ben Jonson, " Gather
ye rose-buds while ye may," in Herrick,
and in Waller's " Go, lovely rose " : —

Was wilt du, Doris, machen?
Brich deinen stolzen geist!
Diss, was du schönheit heist,
Sind blumen-gleiche sachen,
Die unbeständig sind,
Und fliehen wie der wind.

Es wird auf deinen wangen
Nicht steter frühling seyn;
Es weicht der sternen schein,
Als wie der blumen prangen.
Die Zeit, so alles bricht
Schont auch des leibes nicht.

Was ist der schönheit gläntzen,
Als ein geschwinder Blitz?
Sein zubereiter sitz
Besteht in engen gräntzen.
Kein fluss verrauscht so bald,
Als schönheit und gestalt.

Was heute purpur träget,
Und alabaster führt,
Was sich mit rosen ziert,
Wird morgen hingeleget,
Und ruhet ungeacht
In seiner todes-nacht.

Nun, Doris, lerne kennen,
Was falscher hochmuth sey,
Bleib nicht alleine frey,
Lass deine jugend brennen,
Und lass der liebe glut,
Durchwandern hertz und blut.

Gebrauche deine schätze
Weil blut und blüte siegt;
Wann dich die Zeit betrügt
So trennet auch das netze,
So vormahls um dich hieng
Und manche seele fieng.

> So du dich selbst kanst lieben,
> So nimm die Warnung an,
> Die ich dir itzt gethan :
> Ich werde mich betrüben,
> So diese rose stirbt
> Und ohne lust verdirbt."

Certainly it is easy to see, from the successful poems of this period, what it was that their writers tried to express, and this is something that in English at least has made the time memorable for graceful and charming work. It is not surprising, when we recall the political and social condition of Germany, that the poets accomplished less there, yet they did much that was certainly noteworthy, although they are best known for some of the extravagances which were inherent in their zeal for curious conceits. For every literary method, however excellent, carries within it the seeds of decay. Absolute perfection cannot be found; good taste means simply that there is such a thing as bad taste; eloquence implies the existence of bombast, just as we should call nothing tall if there were not shorter things with which comparison is made. The boldness of the Elizabethan drama soon degenerated into a hollow imitation of grandeur; the correctness of the school of Pope into an arid, juiceless precision; and perhaps in our own day we are occasionally thrilled by ingenuities of rhetoric which we mistake for poetical wonders. The fault is, however, more obvious in the past, after it has been definitely determined by universal agreement; and it is nowhere more conspicuous than in the inferior work of this school of poets. In their hunt for what was striking, they found much that was trivial. Cowley and Donne, and indeed Herbert, furnish many examples of this tendency. No one showed it more markedly than did Hofman von Hofmanswaldau. Here is a gem in proof:—

ABRISS EINES FALSCHEN FREUNDES.

Was ist doch ingemein ein Freund in dieser welt?
Ein Spiegel der vergrösst und fälschlich schöner
    machet,

Ein Pfennig der nicht Strich und nicht Gewichte
    hält;
Ein Wesen, so aus Zorn und bittrer Galle lachet,
    Ein Strauehstein, dessen Glantz uns Schand' und
    Schaden bringt;
Ein Glas, an Tituln gut, und doch mit Gifft erfüllet,
    Ein Doleh, der sehreckend ist, und uns in Hertzen
    dringt, —
Ein Heilbrunn (wie er heisst), aus dem Verderben
    quillet,
    Ein goldgestiekter Strang, der uns die Gurgel brieht;
Ein Freund, der ohngefehr das Hertze hat verlohren,
    Ein Honigwurm, der stets mit süssem Stachel sticht;
Ein weisses Hennency, das Drachen-hat gebohren,
    Ein falseher Crocodil, der weinend uns zerreist;
Ein recht Sirenen-Weib, das singend uns erträneket,
    Ein Safft, der lieblich reucht, und doch die Haut
    durchbeist,
Ein Mann, der uns umhalst, wenn seine Hand uns
    heneket,
    Ein Gifftbaun voller Bluth, ein Moloch Musieant;
Ein übergoldte Perl, ein Lock-ass zu den Nöthen,
    Ein Apfel von Damase, ein falscher Diamant;
Ein überzuekert Gifft, ein Irrlicht, uns zu tödten,
    Ein Pfeiffer in das Zarn, ein Spötter unser Pein;
Ein göldner Urtels-Tisch und eine faule Stütze,
    Ein Zeug, der bald versehleist, ein ungregündter
    Schein,
Dem Teuffel allzuschr, dem Menschen wenig nütze.
    Ein mehres lässt mir jetzt die Ungedult nicht zu;
Mein Leser, fleuch den Krahm von solchen falschen
    Waaren,

Was diesen Eifer-Reim erprest, das meide du;
Ach, hätt' ich, was ich schrieb, nicht auch zugleich
  erfahren!

Lohenstein (1635–1683), who wrote tragedies that outdo in horrors what his contemporary accomplished in conceits, is another example of the same school. Andreas Gryphius also wrote tragedies, but under the soothing and chastening influence of Vondel, the Dutch tragedian.

What we notice first, on thinking over the work of such writers, is the inevitableness of a change, and the change soon came; it appeared about simultaneously in England and Germany; and here it was that what is properly called French influence first asserted itself. It also took another and strictly national form in the hands of Christian Weise and others, but the main direction lay in obedience to French taste.

Canitz (1654–1699) was among the first to write in this new fashion. He began with imitating the idols of his time, just as Dryden did in his early poems; but he soon, like his greater English contemporary, gave in his allegiance to the doctrine of Boileau. His satirical poems are inspired by the French writer, and his constant aim was to use poetry as an expression of reason applied to life. Then, too, he wrote a number of occasional poems, like Dryden's elegies, which, in their day, won great admiration. Besser and König carried this method to ludicrous excess. König, for example, in a poem called "Heldenlob Friedrich August's," said: —

Kaum hast du dich vermählt, so heisst ein Zug nach
    Ehren
Dich nach Italien zum zweiten Male kehren,
Die Welschen mussten da beschämt vor Dir gestehen,
Dass selbst ihr altes Reich dergleichen nie gesehen
Und glaubten, weil sie Dich so höchst vollkommen
    fanden,
Dass alle Helden Roms in Dir, Held, auferstanden.

or, to borrow from Hettner again, in his "August im Lager," König described the meeting between the kings of Poland and Prussia: —

Der Ritter edle Schaar vom weissen Adlerorden,
Die über dreissig stark damals gezählet worden,
Sie wurden hingeführt, die von der Kriegesart,
Von unserm Feldmarschall, dem tapfern Wacker-
    barth,
Die aber ihren Dienst dem Hof und Staat erwiesen,
Vom Oberkammerherrn, dem wohlgesinnten Friesen.
Der Ordensadler blitzt mit manchem Demanstein,
Ihr Brustband schliest das Wort mit güldnen Strahlen
    ein :
Den Glauben, das Geseltz, den König zu verfechten.
Das blaue breite Band hängt links ab zu der Rechten,
Der Aufschlag ihres Rocks ist weder lang noch breit,
Der Degengurt gestickt als wie ihr Ordenkleid.

Canitz avoided these lapses of taste, but the "Zeitgeist" revenged itself upon him in the edition of his works which his admirer König brought out; in the prefatory memoir the editor says that Prussia contends with the Mark the honor of being Canitz's birthplace, just as seven Grecian cities contended that Homer was born in them. "But," he goes on, "while the birthplace of the Greek bard is still doubtful, the reader of this memoir will already have perceived that the Freiherr von Canitz, although he sprang from the noble race of Prussian Canitzes, yet was not born in Prussia, or brought up there, and, in the whole course of his life, went there but once, in the campaign of the Kurfürst Friedrich Wilhelm. Consequently Bulen has the sole claim for this honor" (p. 97 ff.). The same genial friend thus describes Canitz's poetry: "His thoughts, like his expressions, bear indubitable witness to his noble education, his knowledge of the world, his associations (Zutritt) with great people, his intimacy with the court, his familiar intercourse with the highest councillors of state, and his acquaintance with the most learned and intelligent men of his time." In short, he was a court poet, and thus he could write, in some lines on the death of the Kurfürstinn Henriette, the wife of him who was later Friedrich I: —

Es konnten Ihren Leib nicht stand noch Jugend retten.

Again we see another curious instance of the all-pervadingness of etiquette in Besser's Ehren-Mahl der Frau von Canitz, in which the bereaved husband is told: —

> Sag'ich : du solltest dich besinnen,
>   Was noch für Trost dein Leiden hat,
>   Das Beyleid dieser gantzen Stadt,
> Ja zweyer grossen Churfürstinnen,
>   Sprichst du : ein Trost von solcher Höh
> Rechtfertige vielmehr dein Weh.

This was the poem in which the writer found it impossible to express to his own satisfaction the thought that the sneer about women first bringing trouble into the world was only true of their death. He wrote to Canitz, who sent him two alternative stanzas; but, meanwhile, Besser had hit on something that pleased Canitz better than either of them.

In his satire on poetry Canitz is very severe on the extravagances of his contemporaries: —

Geht wo ein Schul Regent in einem Flecken ab,
Mein Gott, wie rasen da die Dichter um sein Grab;

Der Tod wird ausgefilzt, dass er dem theueren Leben
Nicht eine längere Frist als achtzig Jahr gegeben ;
　　Die Erde wird bewegt, im Himmel Lerm gemacht.
　　Minerva, wenn sie gleich, in ihrem Hertzen lacht,
Auch Phöbus und sein Chor, die müssen wider willen,
Sich traurig, ohne Trost, in Flor und Boy verhüllen
　　Mehr Götter sieht man offt auf solcem Zettel stehn,
　　Als Bürger in der That mit zu der Leiche gehen."

It is Boileau done over into smooth and readable German. In the little lyrics of this school we find the same ingenious smirk that is to be found in the songs of Sedley, Congreve, etc. A single example will illustrate this; it is from Besser: —

　　Climene starb, und sprach in Scheiden :
　　　"Nun Lisis, nun verlass, ich dich !
　　Ish stürbe willig und mit Freuden,
　　　Liebt' eine dich, so sehr als ich "
　　" Ach," sprach er, " mag dich das betrüben ?
　　　Climene, nur dein Tod ist schwer:
　　Kanst du mich selbst nicht länger lieben,
　　　Bedarf ich keiner Liebe mehr."

There is no need of going through each one of the men who speedily fell into line and acquired the French drill, cutting their verses after the new pattern, and expres-

sing with considerate uniformity monotonous sentiments. The most striking
exception is Johann Christian Günther
(1695–1723), a real poet, who paid dearly
for living in a time of miserable artificiality. His career was one of vice and suffering. His hand was against every man,
and every man's hand was against him.
He uttered the severest denunciations of
his contemporaries, and not the conventional literary abuse that was as artificial
as the love-songs of the time, but genuine
heart-felt wrath, like what we find in Burns.
One of the saddest things in the poor
fellow's career was this: that want compelled him to offer his pen to patrons who
might want a poem turned off at a few
hours' notice. Let us remember, however,
that independence was then impossible; a
poet had to choose between patrons and
starvation. While the other bards were
paying compliments to woman that were
as artificial as the paintings on fans, Gün-

ther wrote the story of his love in verses
that are full of real feeling: —

> In den Wäldern will ich irren,
> Vor den Menschen will ich fliehn,
> Mit verwaysten Tauben girren,
> Mit verscheuchten Wilde ziehn,
> Bis der Gram mein Leben raube
> Bis die Kräffte sich verschreyn:
> Und da soll ein Grab von Laube
> Milder als dein Hertze seyn!

Notice, too, the simplicity of these lines
in a poem about his youth: —

> Die Nachbarskinder liessen mir
> Die Ehre, sie zu lencken;
> Da spielt: und lacht: und sprungen wir
> Auf Rasen, Berg: und Bäncken.
> Was dieser hört und jener sah,
> Das in der grossen Welt geschah,
> Das sucht auch ich mit vielen
> Im kleinen nach zu spielen.

And the despair of this: —

> Nun, leiber Gott, du bleibst ja lange,
> Ich weiss nicht, was ich denken soll.
> Der Zweifel macht der Hoffnung bange,
> Ich weine Bett und Bibel voll;
> Ach, soll denn ich nur ich allein
> Ein Gräuel meines Schöpfers sein!

Was helfen mich nun alle Gaben!
Verstand und Kunst und Ehrlichkeit!
O hätt' ich nur mein Pfund vergraben! .
Es wäre doch wohl eine Zeit,
Indem man aller Orten siehet
Wie hoch der Thoren Glücke blühet.

Die Strafe bessert sonst die Sünder:
Dies ist mehr Grausamheit als Zucht!
Versuch' einmal und geh gelinder,
Vielleicht gewinnt es eher Frucht:
Ein scharfer Streich und langer Grimm
Macht oft die besten Herzen schlimm.

I have spoken of the striking resemblance that Günther bears to Burns; and, inasmuch as, too often, comparisons of this sort are dangerous, because they save thought instead of encouraging it, it may be well to point out a few proofs of this similarity. This first strikes us in the form of the poems, and next in the unhappiness of the lives of both. Günther wrote his lyrical pieces not after the artificial pattern of his day, but to express his real emotions, and the form he chose was that of the "Volkspoesie." He stands as one of the two men of this period who were able to keep true to the traditions of an earlier and less sophisticated method. The other was Paul Fleming, a contemporary of Opitz, who was rewarded with neglect for his indifference to the new elegance of modern verse. Günther felt the intellectual kinship, and wrote about himself: —

Es dörffte mir ein Freund noch manch Gedächtniss
    weihn,
Ich wurd' im Tode mehr, als jetzt im Leben, seyn :
Der stille Rosen-Thal ergetzte meinen Schatten,
Und lässt sich ihn vielleicht mit Flemmings Geiste
    gatten.

Burns brought into modern literature all the charm of the old songs and ballads. He did not invent these, we must remember; he had behind him many generations of verse-loving Scotchmen; he was the final flower, and the poet we are too apt to regard as standing alone by the unaided force of his genius, forgetting that no genius, however brilliant, can accomplish anything without having behind it a vast mass of

effort which too often lacks all recognition
by posterity. In the same way, Flemming
keeps touch with the popular poetry before
Opitz petrified verse by the pedantic rules
that ran over the whole of Europe. Günther, too, wrote verses with the same
charm; and, in explanation of this fact, it
may be possible to suggest that, inasmuch
as he wrote many songs to be sung by his
fellow-students, it was to the preservation,
among these upholders of tradition, of the
" Volkspoesie," that is due his adoption of
this method.[1] Even now, among student-
songs, there survive possibly the " Lauriger
Horatius," and certainly the " Gaudeamus
Igitur,"[2] as indubitable reminiscences of the
carmina burana of the Middle Ages ; and
while the students composed verses after the

---

[1] Something of the kind is hinted at by Erich Schmidt in
his " Komödien vom Studentenleben aus dem sechzehnten
und siebzehnten Jahrhundert " (Leipzig, 1880), p. 21.

[2] *Vide* Creizenach " Die Aeneis, die vierte Ecloge, und
die Pharsalia im Mittelalter," Frankfurt-a-M., 1864, p. 16,
note 91, and Pernwerth von Barnstein, " Ubi sunt qui ante
nos in mundo fuere? " Würzburg, 1881, pp. 104 and 133.

prevailing taste, when they wished to give proof of their accomplishments, they sang for their own delight after the older models. A moment's reflection will make clear the assertion that students are upholders of tradition; the now obsolescent hazing, the drinking customs of German societies, carry the sociologist back to a remote past. Günther's lyrics have at least the charm of vividness, and it is by no means impossible to believe that there survived in private life in Germany a spring of song which even the abundant culture of pseudo-classicism did not extirpate, though it hid it from observation. This was what fed Günther, as, nearly a century later, it inspired Burns, who sang songs to be sung, not merely songs to be criticised and read.

And Günther's life shows the misery that surely awaits the man who is bold enough to tell his generation the things that only the next generation shall delight to hear. Fleming, too, in spite of his superior

poetic power, sang to deaf ears. Günther's
career was one of wretched failure, — partly,
to be sure, from his own fault; but these
faults were in some measure the result of
his perception of his unsuitability for the
artificial work that was demanded of him.
Wretched rhymesters like König and
Besser were at the top of the wave, and it
was almost a century before he received
anything like proper recognition, although
there was an undercurrent of admiration for
him among the people whose voice is never
heard in public. His life, like that of Blake,
Collins, Gray, even Burns, shows how
terrible is the fate of the poet who lives in
an unpoetic age. To win temporary success he must bow to the literary taste of
the day, however artificial it may be, as, to
avoid being mobbed in the streets, he must
wear the dress of the period.

Günther was far removed from the path
which poetry was then to follow, although
dim signs of a change soon began to show

themselves. We have seen hitherto the indications of scarcely anything but the French influence; that of England began very gradually at about this time to make itself felt. When reason was laying its cold hand on poetry, in Germany as well as in England little indications of revolt began to make their appearance. To speak of Brockes as the maker of an epoch seems like a misuse of language. He was the most humdrum of mortals; his statement of the influences that led him to the composition of verse might be a description of the way in which he undertook to pick up horseshoes. The poems themselves are excessively monotonous and often ludicrous, but they conveyed a novelty to readers tired of argument in verse, and had an influence wholly disproportionate to their rhetorical merit. Yet, if we remember that what is said for the first time must be ill said, and that only practice can give anything like perfection, we shall cease to be surprised.

The head waters of the mightiest river are petty enough; we can step over the spring from which it rises without an effort; and, as it would be a hasty notion of physical geography to suppose that the Mississippi flows in its full, broad majesty from a gorgeous grotto, so it is with intellectual movements, which start from obscure corners: it would be a great blunder to expect always to trace them back to grand and dignified beginnings. Yet such is the mistaken notion of the dæmonic splendour of genius, that half of us are amazed to find that the splendour is only a later accompaniment, and has nothing to do with the humble beginning. Indeed, it is a question whether praise and blame, admiration and contempt, have anything whatsoever to do with literary history. Our sole aim should be to know, and as invariably any expression of surprise is nothing more than a confession of ignorance, our blame can merely come from a lack of knowledge of all the facts, and the same must be true of our praise. The highest quality of human nature is comprehension, which is a placid quality. Comprehension of Brockes, at any rate, confers placidity. The humble bard devoted himself to singing the wonders of nature and pointing out how they redounded to the credit of their Creator. This task he performed with cloying profusion, in his "Irdisches Vergnügen in Gott." He seems to have taken for his text the canticle, "O all ye works of the Lord, bless ye the Lord; praise Him, and magnify Him for ever." He gazes into the "sapphire depth of the firmament," "die weder Grund, noch Strom, noch Ziel, noch End' umschrenckt," and "mein ganzes Wesen ward ein Staub, ein Punkt, ein Nichts.

Und ich verlor mich selbst. Diss schlug mich plötzlich
    nieder;
Verzweiflung drohete der ganz verwirrten Brust,
Allein, O heylsam Nichts! glückseliger Verlust!
Allgegenwärt'ger Gott, in dir fand ich mich wieder."

He gazes at the cherry-blossom at night,
"beim Mondenschein," and this, be it said,
is about the first rising of that German
moon which is not yet set. "Ich glaubt es
könne nichts von grösser Weisse seyn. Es
schien ob wär ein Schnee gefallen."

Ein jeder, auch der kleinste Ast
Trug gleichsam eim schwere Last
Von zierlich weissen runden Ballen.
Es ist kein Schwan so weiss, da nemlich jedes Blatt,

Indem daselbst des Mondes sanftes Licht
Selbst durch die zarten Blätter bricht,
Sogar den Schatten weiss and sonder Schwärze hat,
Unmöglich, dacht' ich, kan auf Erden
Was weissers angetroffen werden.

The upshot of this genuine outburst of
admiration is that it occurred to him, —

Wie sehr ich mich am Irdischen ergetze,
Dacht' ich, hat Gott dennoch weit grössre Schätze,
Die grösste Schönheit dieser Erden
Kann mit der Himmlischen doch nicht verglichen
       werden.

The same appreciative eye was turned to
the ant, to various flowers in his garden, to

the early buds on his pear-tree, which inspire him with this pious assurance of
security: —

Ach warum soll denn ich mit kindlichem Vertrauen
Auf deiner Lieb' und Vater-Treu nicht bauen,
In fester Zuversicht, Du werdest hier, im Leben
Den'n meinigen und mir leicht Kost and Kleider geben.

In winter he assures his Creator that devotion is not frozen out of him: —

Mein Gott! das Feuer wärmet mich
Und macht mich nur, dass ich nicht friere;
Dass ich im Frost auch Anmuth spüre
Dafür erheb' und preis' ich dich!
  Ich fühl' jetzt einen Trieb in mir,
Ein Winter-Opfer dir zu bringen,
Und deim Wunder zu besingen
Die ich, auch selbst im Frost, verspühr.

Even in the contemplation of the wolf
he finds material for spiritual edification: —

Sind auch in Wölfen viele Dinge zu unseren
Nutzen noch zu finden; Wir haben nicht nur ihrer
Bälge im scharfen Frost uns zu erfreuen, Es dienen
ihrer Glieder viele zu grossem Nutz in Arzeneien.

Another instance may be taken from the
chamois, and it may well stand as prose: —

Für die Schwindsucht ist ihr Unschlitt, fürs Gesicht die Galle gut; Gemsenfleisch ist gut zu essen, und den Schwindel heilt ihr Blut; Auch die Haut dient uns nicht minder; strahlet nicht aus diesem Thier nebst der Weisheit und der Allmacht auch des Schöpfers Lieb hervor?

Yet less valuable than these raptures would be ridicule of them, and beneath the moral lessons which were part of the tribute he paid to the spirit of his day,— as ridicule would be our tribute to the spirit of our day,— we may see that his eye was detecting a novel solemnity in what modern science was making known to the world. The telescope and microscope were widening the field of the emotions. While Brockes was exhaling in verse the raptures he felt over the " Punckten-förmigen Gestalt der Himmels-Lichter," which gave him " sichere Schlüsse," and he felt that " ich selber etwas grosses bin," and while in the blue firmament there was detected,—

Ein ewiges, allgegenwärtig's all,
Ein unermess'lichs Ganz, in dem, als wie ein Ball

Im weiten Ocean, nicht nur die Erd'allein,
Nein, ein unzählbar Herr von Sonnen, Sternen, Erden,
Dir bloss durch ihn umringt, erfällt, erhalten werden,
In stiller Majestät, in reger Ruhe schwimmt.

Addison, in the *Spectator*, was saying very nearly the same thing in prose: —

But when we survey the whole earth at once, and the several planets that lie within its neighborhood, we are filled with a pleasing astonishment to see so many worlds hanging one above another, and sliding round their axles in such an amazing pomp and solemnity. (No. 420.)

Again (No. 565): —

Were the sun, which enlightens the part of the creation, with all the host of planetary worlds that move about him, utterly extinguished and annihilated, they would not be missed more than a grain of sand upon the sea shore. . . . In this consideration of God Almighty's omnipresence and omniscience every uncomfortable thought vanishes. He cannot but regard everything that has being, especially such of his creatures who fear they are not regarded by him, *etc.*

It is easy to understand how these discoveries rendered men discontented with the narrow limitations that had previously impressed themselves on human thought and feelings. The spirit of rationalism appeared inevitably when the rigidity of old superstitions was broken; man assumed new importance by the side of which conventions of royalty and aristocracy were insignificant, and the new thought of the eighteenth century may be dated from this widening of men's knowledge. Yet there are those who lament the depressing effect that science has upon letters. Is literature, then, a superstition that must shun the light?

In Brockes the new feeling was often expressed in a way that now seems grotesque. When he began to observe his emotions of delight he confounded them in a most unconventional way. We have seen with what delight he gazed at the white blossoms in the moonlight, and how he expressed his pleasure as a Chinese or Japanese poet might do until he brought up with his moral, but in these lines we find him without a rival: —

> Ach welche Sussigkeit!
> Welch ausserlich und innerlichs Ergetzen
> Empfindet man bey stiller Abend-Zeit,
> Wenn wir den müden Leib auf weichen Feder-
> Decken,
> Mit einigen Erwegen strecken!

Yet even here, as Brandl has well said in his monograph on Brockes,[1] these Philistine lines are a natural consequence of his way of regarding humanity. Invariably selection is something later than the first feeling. Brockes also translated Pope's "Essay on Man" in 1740, and Thomson's "Seasons" in 1745. Some of the extracts that are given above will show his indebtedness to English models; and, like them, he endeavored to teach how every man might make better use of his senses, a lesson that he will be credited with teaching the Germans.

Haller (1708–1777) was a man of far

---

[1] Page 65.

more importance. He began, to be sure, under the inspiration of Lohenstein and what is called the second Silesian school, following the unwritten law in accordance with which almost every writer first pays allegiance to fading authorities, and is even more old-fashioned than his adult contemporaries; but the influence of the philosophical English poetry, especially that of Pope, soon led him to writing after their own method. His long poem on the Origin of Evil is one of this sort; but his "Die Alpen" is the one on which his poetical fame now rests, although the "Ode to Eternity" possibly touches a higher chord. The poem on the Alps describes the majesty of mountain scenery with an eloquence that had no precedent. To be sure, the poet reminds us at times that —

——der Himmel has diess Land noch mehr geliebet,
Wo nichts, was nöthig, fehlt, und nur was nützet,
    blüht,
Der Berge wachsend Eis, der Felse steile Wände
Sind selbst zum Nützen da, und tränken das Gelände.

and when —

senkt ein kahler Berg die glatten Wände nieder
. . . . .
Nicht fern vom Eise streckt, voll futterreicher Weide,
Ein fruchtbares Gebürg den breiten Rücken her,
Sein sanfter Abhang glänzt von reifendem Getreide,
Und seine Hügel sind von Hundert Herden schwer.

Yet he has an eye at times for the scenery
alone, apart from the fertility of the soil: —

Hier zeigt ein steiler Berg die mauergleichen Spitzen,
Ein Waldstrom eilt hindurch, und sturzet Fall auf Fall,
Der dickbeschäumte Fluss dringt durch der Felsen
　　　　Ritzen,
Und schiesst mit gäher Kraft weit über ihren Wall.

And before this: —

Wenn Titans erster Strahl der gipfel Schnee vergüldet,
ˈUnd sein verklärter Blick die Nebel unterdrückt,
So wird, was die Natur am prächtigsten gebildet,
Mit immer neuer Lust von einem Berg erblickt.

Still, after all, it is rather the pleasant
valleys than the steep mountains that catch
his eye. Yet it is to Haller's credit that
he was not, like most of his contemporaries,
simply repelled by the savage gloom of the

mountains. After all, while he belonged
to his generation, as these extracts show,
he was yet raised above them by his position as a man of science to whom everything appealed; and in this poem he indicated — though confusedly — the direction
in which taste was about to move. We
notice this more especially in his picture
of the Arcadian simplicity of the Swiss.
He made the same comparison between
their innocence and the corruption of the
civilized world that, nearly half a century
later, Rousseau eloquently presented to his
fascinated readers. This fact gives the
poem a most important position in literary
history; for, while what he said about the
scenery is more truly an indication than
an expression of our later raptures, his
accounts of the idyllic life of the Swiss
clearly foreboded Gellert and Rousseau. In
England James Thomson, as Taine says,[1]

[1] "History of English Literature." New York: 1861,
i. 219.

"thirty years before Rousseau, had expressed all Rousseau's sentiments, almost in the same style." He, too, compared the corruptions of modern times with the innocent past, and the vicious city with the idyllic country. He was among the first to sing the beauty of nature, and it is curious to observe that he was a contemporary of Haller, as well as a fellow-worker. Thomson began his "Liberty" in 1731, and the first parts of it appeared in 1734. Haller's "Die Alpen" was written in 1729 and published in 1732. The "Seasons" was completed by 1730. Thus, we see the simultaneous appearance in Switzerland and England of the spirit that was to destroy the current thought; and possibly, in time, the discovery of other alleged coincidences of this sort will be of service in dispelling the notion that the study of literature has no scientific value.

Haller's longer philosophical poems have often aroused discussion as to whether or

not Haller should be regarded as a direct
imitator of Pope, with whom he became a
fellow-worker as he had been of Thomson.
The question need not detain us long. It
is only our duty to remember that the
whole matter of plagiarism is in a very
crude state. If we look at the subject
fairly, we shall see at once that any man
who is abreast with his generation, who has
been exposed to the same influences as his
contemporaries, will probably see the next
step that the processes of thought demand
to be taken in just the same way as some
one else will see it. Hence, when we find,
at similar stages of culture throughout
Europe, different races repeating one another's experiences, we shall observe that
the instinct of imitation is far from being
the sole cause of the similarity of their
actions. Men in England and men in Germany find similar solutions for the same
problems, because they have the same ma-
terials for devising an answer. Pope had

been moved by Shaftesbury and Leibnitz in writing his "Essay on Man;" and Haller, another cultivated man, was inspired by Shaftesbury and Leibnitz in writing his philosophical poetry. That there was a likeness between the work of the two men is certainly less surprising than would be its absence. We may expect to find the men of an army near together and acting with some uniformity when they are making their way through woods or fording a stream; and every generation is, as it were, an army that is doing its best to conquer the world. Some are skirmishers in advance, and some are laggards in the rear; the majority are in a monotonous mass, keeping touch with one another, and moving in one uniform direction, with the skirmishers only a little in advance and resting on the main body.

In Hagedorn (1708–1754) we have a poet whose importance the literary historians of Germany are never tired of pointing out.

He it was who brought into repute some of
the forms of verse that were much admired
in France and England, and remained popular in Germany until — it is scarcely too
much to say — poets found that they had
really a message to deliver. Hagedorn in-
troduced in their modern form the lyric, the
fable, and the poetic tale. Primarily, all of
these modes of expression were French; yet
in England they flourished in the hands of
Prior, Swift, and Gay; while in Germany
they all, but especially the fable, developed
in a slightly different way. It was doubtless this novel urbanity, familiar enough
elsewhere, but strange here, that gave
Hagedorn his fame.

CHAPTER III.

WHILE the doors were thus opened to English influence in poetry, English prose was also entering into Germany, as we see by the numberless imitations of "Robinson Crusoe," that speedily appeared after the translation of the unsurpassed original. While all that has been hitherto described belongs to the history of what was distinctly a literary class, the Robinsonaden, as they were called, were a part of popular literature. They amalgamated with the stories that appeared after the Thirty Years' War, which were reminiscences of imitations of the Spanish picaresque tales; and, although crude and slight, they yet showed, as well as furthered, the general interest in something adventurous and foreign. The English "Robinson Crusoe" was a coherent part of the busy, roaming, active English life; the German imitations had, too often, as vague a background of reality as have Jules Verne's stories. And, as Karl Elze has pointed out,[1] it was in the inland countries that most of them were written, and not in the maritime towns. The best of them all, "The Swiss Family Robinson," had its birthplace far from saltwater.

Much more important were the English essays, the "Spectator," etc., which immediately called forth a number of German imitations. I have shown elsewhere the steps by which the English originals acquired the form by which they are still well known to us, and which for a century was a favorite method of conveying amusement and instruction to the public. In Germany they were equally popular, though, as was to be expected, of far less literary merit.

[1] "Die Englische Sprache und Literatur in Deutschland." Dresden: 1864, p. 41.

They at present concern us as the weapons
with which was fought out the contest
between French and English influence in
Germany. We have already seen the
modest beginnings of French authority in
the satiric and courtly poems of Canitz and
others; but this asserted itself most strongly
in the work of Gottsched, who was the
most prominent figure in the literature of
the first half of the eighteenth century, and
the most ludicrous in the eyes of men since
that period. This subsequent contempt is
the price he has paid for the adoration he
received in his lifetime for giving the most
complete expression to the taste of his con- ·
temporaries. Yet of late he is receiving in
some measure fuller justice from those
writers of literary history who perceive
that he did but carry the Germans through
an inevitable stage of their progress. Ridicule of his lessons is certainly a barren
method: one might as well laugh at a tree
for shedding its leaves in autumn, as at the

Germans for obeying an influence that overwhelmed the whole of civilized Europe.

Gottsched was born in 1700, and, after completing his studies in Königsberg, he made his way to Leipzig, which was then distinctly a literary centre. Its book trade put the town into direct communication with the whole of Germany. Already a society existed since 1697 which was devoted to the study of the German language, and of this Gottsched was soon made a member. In this society he at once became prominent; he got its name changed from the "Deutschübende Gesellschaft" to the "Deutsche Gesellschaft;" and it at once became the model of a number of similar varieties in different parts of Germany. The new non-resident members and the related societies united in recognizing Gottsched's importance, and he found himself in a position of great influence. He maintained himself here by untiring labor, and it is easy to see how much good work

lay beneath much that posterity has agreed
to condemn. His first efforts were in a
humble sphere. He wrote book after book
on rhetoric, grammar, eloquence, the art of
verse; he gave precision to the confused
unsettled usage of the German tongue, and
thus met the generally felt need of a common means of communication among other
classes than the learned; for in Germany, as
in England, after the revolution of 1688,
the *bourgeoisie* was beginning to interest
itself in literature.[1] It was gradually losing
interest in the impossible romances that had
given the intensest pleasure not many years
before, and which still lingered as the favorite reading of the ignorant and of children. In both countries there existed a
strong yearning for moral and social instruction. The essayists soon undertook to
provide this, and Gottsched soon established

---

[1] *Vide* Julian Schmidt, "Geschichte des geistigen Lebens
in Deutschland von Leibnitz bis auf Lessing's Tod." Leipzig: 1862, v. i., 436 ff.

a paper, in imitation of the English "Spectator." The subject that he had nearest at heart was the elevation of German literature, which was certainly an honourable ambition; and he made a discreet choice in selecting the drama as the means best suited for bringing literature into close relation with the life of the people. To be sure, we now can see the certain failure of the artificial alliance which he endeavoured to establish; but, in selecting the French stage for his model, he did the only thing which it was possible for him to do. It is idle to condemn Gottsched for this choice, inasmuch as there was actually no alternative before him. When even in England, with Shakespeare and his fellow-workers to inspire opposition to the French influence, the whole current ran for a time in this direction, there is no need for wondering that Gottsched accepted what was most successful for his model. Moreover, the attempt to revive the German drama, which at the best had never flourished, and had sunk to a wretched depth, would have been hopeless; and, in adopting French models, Gottsched, it is further to be noted, also lent his encouragement to the general desire for moral teaching. Dr. Johnson, in the preface to his Shakespeare, lamented that poet's indifference to right and wrong and to "opportunities of instructing and delighting," and that he wrote "without any moral purpose," comparing him unfavorably in this respect with the later writers of the English tragedy; and in Racine's later plays, piety had asserted itself with noticeable earnestness. Consequently, in doing his best to expel grossness and roughness from the German stage, Gottsched had the double consolation of encouraging good morals as well as good letters. Addison must have known the same feeling when he wrote his "Cato" to fill the place of the extravagant heroic plays. He at once began to translate, with the aid of his wife and children, the most celebrated French tragedies, and soon found encouragement in the success of the actors, who were readily induced to take an interest in this new venture. His own play, " Der sterbende Cato," modelled on Addison's Cato, and one by Deschamps, was one of many examples of the readiness of the Germans. The German opera was driven away, and the equivalent of the English clown was finally banished from the stage. It has been given to few literary autocrats to attain anything like his success. His ambition did not stop here; he sought to extend his domain over the whole realm of poetry; but he very soon met with opposition. We shall soon see how the carefully constructed theory of the drama fell into ruins; but, before that crash, Gottsched was engaged in a bitter controversy regarding the true meaning of poetry, his antagonists being two Swiss writers, Bodmer (1698–1783) and Breitinger (1701–1776). It is worthy

of note that his opponents lived in Switzerland, a country that had been saved from
some of the movements of modern taste by,
one may fairly say, its physical geography.
For mountains do not merely protect those
who live near them from the winds of
heaven that sweep unbroken over the level
plain; they serve as a barrier in the path
of travellers; they destroy readiness of
communication; and, as we find old-fashioned dresses in their seclusion, and the phil-
ologist lights on idioms forgotten elsewhere,
so the thoughts of the people were to some
extent preserved from the influence of principles that have full sway elsewhere. In
Zürich, which belonged to the Protestant
part of Switzerland, there existed at the
beginning of the last century a general
interest in letters. Its exceptional political
and religious condition secured for it the
same freedom in forming intellectual alli-
ances that is given to us Americans at the
present day, and led it naturally to an

interest in England, where there existed similar political freedom and religious zeal. Moreover, the prominence of England in science attracted to it the attention of students, just as all serious workers now follow German methods.

Bodmer and Breitinger were moved by admiration of the "Spectator" to establish a similar publication in Zürich; and Addison's enthusiastic praise of Milton soon found enthusiastic admirers in these two men. Whereas they had begun their literary career by acknowledging Gottsched's supremacy, they soon wandered from the straight and narrow path which he had traced for all lovers of literature; and, as early as 1724, Bodmer had translated the "Paradise Lost," although his version was not published until 1732; and in 1737 he translated Butler's "Hudibras." Although at first Gottsched praised the German translation of Milton's poem, he afterwards took the opposite view, and the contest

between the Swiss and the Leipzig school
soon became bitter. It was in 1740 that the
Zürich leaders opened all their batteries,
and the fray fairly began. That Gottsched
should have opposed any assertion of the
authority of Milton is, when we consider his
literary principles, perfectly natural. It was
not a simple personal choice that decided
him, though possibly he may have thought
so, any more than it is true that a stream
flows to the sea by personal choice. If
its level lies through a sandy region, it
must flow over sand; and it is with equal
inevitableness that Gottsched's theories
hardened his heart against Milton. He
was by no means alone in his opposition.
It will be remembered that the great
English poet had been neglected by his
fellow-countrymen when Addison undertook his resuscitation and proved his ex-
cellence by the use of the weapons of the
very men who condemned his sins against
the poetry of reason. Yet the whole school

of critics, from Rymer to Dr. Johnson, who believed in the principles that animated Gottsched, nourished open or secret opposition to Milton. They believed that rhyme was essential to poetry, and, so believing, they detested blank verse. They liked directness and exactness of speech; Milton's language, with its remote suggestions and majestic harmonies, sinned against this essential necessity. In a word, he was the last of the poets of the inspiration of the Renaissance; they were earnest adherents of the school that aimed at the correction of its predecessors and could in no way admire him. In Germany, as in England, the appreciation of Milton's merits became the test of literary preferences; and, in the discussion that went on, we may see, now that the smoke of the battle is blown away, — a battle in which the amount of powder burned was in no proportion to the size or number of the bullets, — we may see, I say, in the subsequent discussion, how much the inconsistencies with which both sides have been charged were inherent in the principles from which they started. The Swiss critics, in their zeal against Gottsched and all that he represented, asserted that the poet should have nothing to do with what was natural and common, but should describe only what was supernatural and wonderful; and, although they attacked with intelligence the weak points of Gottsched's theory, the best that they could do in constructing a positive theory was to commend fables like Æsop's as a model. Yet it is not merely what a critic positively affirms that inspires those who listen to him. They are moved by the implications which the critic himself may not fully develop; and, in opposing Bodmer and Breitinger, Gottsched was moved by the same detestation of their belief in enthusiasm as was Pope when he made Theobald the main hero of his "Dunciad;" for Theobald had ventured to say, in the preface to his edition of the works of Beaumont and Fletcher, that he thought enthusiasm was the very essence of poetry.

Gottsched, on the other hand, maintained that nothing lay nearer men's interests than human nature, and that experiments with the supernatural must necessarily fail, and were only very seldom allowable. ' Bodmer's "Noachide" (translated into English about 1764) must have seemed to him to have been written to corroborate his views; and even Klopstock's "Messiah" betrays all the weakness of his antagonist; but Gottsched went much further: he had nothing but faint praise for Homer; Milton he detested; Ariosto's poems, he said, were delirious visions, without order or resemblance to truth; Tasso had " such love for devilishness that he jumbled together the mass and litany with conspiracies and magical formulas, heaven with hell, Christianity with paganism and Mohammedan superstition, in the most offensive way,"

etc. Yet it is well, before condemning, to
remember Voltaire's assertion of the superiority of Tasso to Homer, Johnson's
continual contempt for Milton, and the slow
growth in England, among the most cultivated, of Shakespeare's fame. If Gottsched
was more distinctly philistine in his views
than the men of other countries, it must
not be forgotten that the sort of mistake
which he made was but the natural expression of a widespread error. He paid dearly
for living in a rude, unpolished country,
just as his antagonists manifested their provincialism by occasional indiscreet admiration. Gottsched, too, lived long enough to
find his name a byword; to see himself
deserted by every one; and Germany, in
whose behalf he had toiled so arduously,
wholly abandoned to the heresies that he had
fought with tireless zeal. He died in 1766,
the year in which Lessing's "Laocoön"
appeared, and just before the "Hamburger
Dramaturgie" and "Minna von Barnhelm"

made the victory of the new generation complete.

Long before his death, modest preparations were making for the coming change. Some young men who started as Gottsched's disciples gradually freed themselves from his control, and, in the "Bremer Beiträge," devoted their attention to the newer and less rigorous forms of literature. Such were Gärtner, Rabener, Elias Schlegel, Cramer, and others; but their work was of but moderate importance. Gellert, who used the fable as a means of conveying instruction and temperate delight, moved in the same direction; but the fable, the Anacreontic song, the moral tale, and the improving satire, which flourished simultaneously, seem to be more heavily freighted with the past than with the future.

By what they did after these models, the Germans seemed to themselves to be keeping step with the rest of Europe, but it was only in a half-hearted way; and Bodmer eagerly yearned for some one who should write the missing epic in the Miltonic spirit, and thus justify his criticisms as well as complete German literature. At length he found what he had sought in Klopstock (1724–1803), the first three books of whose "Messias" were published in the "Bremer Beiträge" in 1748. At first the poem excited as little interest in Germany as it can now in this country; but Bodmer was fire and flame in admiration, and the story of his relations with its author is one of the more amusing bits of the literary gossip of the last century. That he should have been delighted with the poem explains itself without difficulty; for it at once justified the position he had taken in criticism; it was another tribute to the greatness of Milton, and a proof that his own abstract theories bore the test of practical experiment. In Gottsched's eyes the poem was an abomination; for it tore to pieces the tottering fabric that he had

built with so much care. In his wrath he
picked up a stray heroic poem, von Schön-
aich's "Hermann," that was written by
one of his admirers, and did his best with
this new weapon to drive the pretender
from the field; but his efforts were vain,
and only made the poor man's failure as a
dictator more ridiculous. If this ill-fated
"Hermann" was always unreadable, the
once more fortunate "Messias" has now
certainly become so; but the poem holds a
position in the history of literature which
saves it from obscurity. We see in it many
signs of the new spirit; for, while it drew
much of its inspiration from Milton, this
influence was largely diluted with more
modern tears. As Coleridge said of him,
Klopstock was a very German Milton; and,
in place of a strong handling of a vast subject, we have the emotions that the subject
is capable of calling forth, but nothing else.
His enthusiasm evaporated in sighs. When
he comes to describing anything that calls

for a vivid statement of his own, he tells us
that the incident is ineffable, inexpressible,
and he declines to say more about it. These
are literary objections, and in no way touch
the importance of the poem as an expression of the diffused, if not deep, religious
sentiment of the time. We will readily
recall the existence of the same feeling in
England; and Young's "Night Thoughts,"
Blair's "Grave," and Hervey's "Medita-
tions" all bear witness to its importance.
Yet there is a great difference to be noticed
between the dominant emotions in the two
countries under similar religious excitement.
While the English mainly contemplated
the grave and its horrors, the Germans enjoyed a tearful ecstacy. Young and Blair
are more truly degenerate descendants of
Milton, — of a Milton trimmed to the cool
requirements of the eighteenth century.
Klopstock, on the other hand, is full of
many of the qualities which are at once apparent in the full glory of German litera-

ture in its speedy development. He was
at least enthusiastic, even if we may not
share his enthusiasm; they were cold and
academic. They brought to an end the traditions of Milton, although his blank verse
survived in many didactic poems; but in
Germany, as Hettner has well said, the
"Messiah" brought salvation. The hex-
ameter, in which measure the poem was
written, became a common form in the later
and more skilful hands of Voss and
Goethe; yet this is the slightest of his ser-
vices, — one, it may be added, that had its
origin in Bodmer's advice, which had also
been given by Gottsched a few years
earlier. This fervent use of language was a
complete change from the tepid correctness
that had been the aim of his predecessors,
and continued to be that of some of his
contemporaries. When, in his odes, he
broke loose from rhyme and tried to write
in the measures of the Greek and Roman
classics, he went further than the Germans

have agreed to follow him; but he at least
destroyed the omnipotence of the rigidity
that had previously ruled. It is to be noticed too, that, while Klopstock's earliest
unrhymed odes bear the date of 1747, that
in the same year Collins's " Odes " were
first published, containing the beautiful unrhymed " Ode to Evening." [1] But Collins
sang to deaf ears, while Klopstock was not
only followed by a swarm of short-lived
imitators, but also had considerable influence on many of the most illustrious of his
followers. Just as a lightly laden, easily
handled craft will go about sooner than a
huge ship, so did Germany precede England
in preparation for the coming change.
The bulk of English didactic poetry gave
the literature of that country more head-
way. But its new rival found in Klop-

---

[1] Of course it is not meant that Klopstock was the first to
adopt this form; he was preceded, for example, by Pyra
and Lange, just as there were unrhymed Horatian odes in
English between Milton and Collins, e. g., S. Say's Poems,
p. 79, where may be found one written in 1720.

stock's verse an ally in its struggle to better things. In the first place, the "Messias" was a hopeful poem; while the English religious poems sang solely the gloomy horrors of the unfruitful grave. To be sure, this was lit by the dim light of the moon; but it was the waning, late-rising moon that, after dimly illuminating the romantic novels of Mrs. Radcliffe and her fellow-workers, set in the wild extravagance of now forgotten tragedies like "Bertram," which is only given a taste of immortality by Coleridge's denunciation of it. Klopstock sang with unfamiliar fervour of love and friendship; Bodmer even said of his ode, "Die Braut," that it might have been written by the Messiah himself, had he ever been in love! But Bodmer often allowed himself strange expressions. What Klopstock did was to introduce into German literature the gracious way of writing about women, which had for a long time been absent. He sang of love as a sentiment, and of friendship as a sentiment, and, it may be added, of love of nature as a sentiment. Some of these qualities it is possible to detect — in a crude state, to be sure — in what we know of Bodmer, whose enthusiasms foreboded what Klopstock was about to accomplish. Indeed, the Swiss critic's life is full of the quality that Klopstock knew better as material for poetry than as a rule of conduct. This is proved by his enthusiasm, when a man of fifty, over the young poet, who preferred flirting with the young women of Zürich, and drinking with the young men, to studying Switzerland, and serious devotion to writing. When Bodmer wanted to show Klopstock the distant beauties of the Alps through a spy-glass, he lamented that the younger poet preferred to turn the spy-glass toward the windows of Zürich. Yet this is not the first time or the last that there has been discord between young men and old men, and on this subject; or that a

poet's life has not borne out all that his
verses seemed to indicate. The general
sentimentality of Klopstock's poems found
many ready to condemn it, but more who
were disposed to accept it; for, with the
decay of reasonableness as the inspiration
of poetry, human nature once more asserted
itself, and gave full expression to emotions
that had been temporarily ousted from literature, and, doubtless, to some extent, from
life; for our inclinations and habits are
modified by the ideals that we find in books,
which themselves describe what their
writers see about them. It is scarcely accurate to speak of this sensibility as a new
thing, as is often done. It has been more
than half hidden by the civilization of the
period just disappearing; but, in the remoter past of the heroic novel, tears had
been as frequent a pleasure to the noble
lords and ladies who lived in that fairyland,
as they were destined to be in the age just
beginning. The merest glance at the heroic

novels will confirm this statement, and in
the heroic plays we find equal sensibility;
although in these, at least in the English
ones, there is often a hysteric roar which
hides the susceptibility to tears.[1] In the
letters of Klopstock and of his contemporaries we find abundant traces of this long-
suppressed, emotional sensitiveness. It
had, however, all the charm, and, besides
the charm, the crudity of novelty. The
religious epic, which was a remote outwork
from Milton's greater work, and the poetical
expression of the pietism that had long
existed in Germany, reached its culmination
here, and soon ceased to be a tempting
ideal for a generation that was learning to
disregard religion. In other ways Klopstock was pointing out the future course of
thought. He soon became enthusiastic for

[1] This is well brought out in Fournel's " La Littérature
Indépendante et les Écrivains oubliés au XVII.ᵐᵉ siècle,"
chaps. IV. and V. He makes it very clear that sensibility
cannot be derived from Mme. de Lafayette's " Princesse de
Clèves," as some have thought.

Teutonic subjects; and in his odes, in which the early German deities took the place of those of Greece and Rome, he was breaking the bonds of pseudo-classicism, as well as encouraging the patriotism which, throughout Europe, was destined to take the place of the cosmopolitanism that was growing up under the influence of a monotonous literary culture. Indeed, the cultivation that was formed on Roman models carried with it the *imperium Romanum* in literature. It rested on a widespread and generally accepted basis of common knowledge, with, one might almost say, a common language at its command; for in Spain, as in Russia, Cupid's shafts, Vulcan's lameness, Minerva's wisdom, everywhere brought the same images to those who were continually reading about them. Then the forms of verse were alike throughout all the countries of Europe. The satires reverberated from one end of it to the other. The softer elegies, the didactic poems, the

epigrams, sounded gentler but no less frequent notes. It was as if one language
was spoken in many dialects. That the
French should have been the most stren-
uous supporters of this cosmopolitanism
will not surprise us. These new tendencies
in literature derived their main authority
from France, where the national life had the
least representation in literature, as in politics; and where, too, the national characteristics were those most prominent in this
literary method, such as concinnity and
directness. The French zeal for cosmopolitanism, which implied taking France
for a model, was like Heine's definition
of the French nation of equality, — every
man wanted his superiors brought down
to his level. Every rebellion against the
rigid laws of pseudo-classicism was a
serious matter, and, whenever it broke
out, it found its sole support in an ap-
peal to some of the national distinctions.
It may not be fanciful, however, to conjec-

ture that the Protestant epics had been
attempts in the same direction. Du Bartas,
in France, with his "Semaine," may be
acquitted of overt rebellion, because the
jurisdiction of the classics had not been
firmly established in his time. But Milton,
with his blank verse and grand style, had
stood forth in opposition to the admired
couplet and colourless verse that were
fastening themselves on English poetry, as
Addison saw when he praised him, to the
discomfiture of the unreasonable lovers of
reasonable verse.

Yet Klopstock's patriotism was at first
simple enough, reminding us as it does of
the Americanism of these poets who for
castles write *wigwams*, and for *nightin-
gales, mockingbirds.* There was no Germany to inspire the feeling of patriotism,
but merely a congeries of rival States
speaking the German tongue; yet the feeling that was going to cast these separate .
atoms into a coherent whole began to make

itself felt in this early patriotism. Let us notice one thing about it, which may simplify for us the study of literature, and of much else; and that is, that the way in which every new interest of the human mind first makes its appearance is as the merest sentiment. This may seem an absolute platitude; but, if we examine a moment, it may help to explain some difficulties. And by sentiment I mean what we call sentimentality, which may always be taken to signify a sentiment that in time arouses our distaste. If we seek for a few examples or tests, we shall find the rudimentary, crude feeling in the dim hatred of oppression, which, after lying inert in the hands of the sentimentalists, crystallizes into action in the hands of energetic men. The course of the Abolitionists may prove this: after years of agitation, declamation, and denunciation, the feeling which was first the exclusive property of sentimentalists and the detestation of practical men became a

part of law, and the property of men who
pride themselves on hatred of sentimentality. In the matters more immediately
before us we see the crude feeling for
nature, and apparently idle opposition to
the classes of reasonable poetry, in Brockes,
which only later became a fixed principle,
just as in Poussin and Claude Lorraine we
see the mountains figuring as ornaments of
the background, awaiting the time when
they were to be regarded as themselves
objects of interest. In the works of these
early painters, as Lotheissen has well said,[1]
we find represented the scenery of the fash-
ionable Arcadias and shepherd-romances
which supplied the raw material that was
afterwards to develop into the love of
nature. Another example is the horror of
the romances, beginning with the "Castle
of Otranto," that was to appear as a greater
indulgence in vague mental emotion, and to

[1] Geschichte der französischen Literatur im XVII.ten
Jahrhundert. III., 368 ff.

become a prominent quality in subsequent literature. In the same way we perceive in Klopstock's zeal for the remote past of Germany the early buddings of the romantic revival.

CHAPTER IV.

In Wieland, on the other hand, we see another and very different part of the same movement making its appearance; whereas Klopstock, in his "Messias," sang rather an exalted, vague elevation of the soul, than any definite cosmogony of heaven, and, in his celebration of the early history of Germany, he wrote with an unreality that seems to us confusing. He nevertheless helped to bring to notice what was then a wilderness, but in time became a familiar region. Wieland, who began by following in Klopstock's footprints and composed religious poems, afterwards became famous as the leader of some of the innovations of French and English taste. Klopstock's followers lived in cloudland, and imagined themselves great geniuses on account of

104

the facility with which they imitated the
most obvious faults of the illustrious model.
Wieland, detesting their obscurity and extravagance, devoted himself to glorifying
terrestial grace and charm. His early re-
ligiosity, when he had once recovered from
it, left behind nothing but the familiar
mortification for an exploded enthusiasm.
From singing Platonic love he turned to
singing emotions that were anything but
platonic. Germany appeared to be turning
into a land where the full moon lit lonely
graves, on which sat weeping figures,
mourning only that they were not yet real
spectres. He filled the stage with a band
of revellers, whose sole delight in moonlight was that it did not betray half of their
frivolities, and who made the most of the
life they had. He belonged, indeed, to
those men who, in France and England,
devoted themselves to singing the joys of
the present; who learned from the current
philosophy enough scepticism to doubt

everything but their own perception of the moment. The age was speeding towards the great Revolution, while Wieland was maintaining that men neglected their capacity for material enjoyment. Yet his work was of service, because it tended to make reality important, and to dispel the mists of wild enthusiasm. He was much admired in his day, although now he pays for his ancient fame by persistent neglect. Possibly a good part of the fame that he got came from a feeling of gratitude among the Germans for his success in polishing the language, — in giving it an unwonted grace, — and for proving that the Germans were not really what they had long been supposed to be, — a clumsy race. The fact that he had done this gave him what to foreigners may seem like undue prominence. He becomes historically important; but we are ready to leave untouched his work, which is made up of inspirations drawn from the French, the English, the

Italians, and the later Greek writers. Yet,
besides the undoubted charm of much that
he wrote, we must remember that he stood
forth as the representative of one of the
great currents of thought that existed
throughout Europe before the Revolution.
So much at least is true, that, if we include
his whole life, he followed many currents;
but he is interesting, as an example of the
complete civilization which had no sooner
established itself than it was overthrown,
—as absolutism always must be overthrown, so long as man is a growing creature. The crowning point of the civilization of the last century was a being without
prejudices, who believed only what he saw,
and for whom what he did not see was a
chaos as dark as Central Africa was in the
old atlases. Grace, ease, civilization, —
for that sense of the word survives, although the fact is gone, and words, being
born later, live longer than the facts, —
all combined to make the last half of the

eighteenth century one of those periods
when perfection shone in this dull, clumsy,
stupid world; and we turn back to it with
that feeling which we always have for perfection, whether it be shown in strength,
or pathos, or charm; whether in villainy
or virtue, so long as it is our neighbor
who suffers and not ourselves. It was then
that the cultivation of the Renaissance cul-
minated; the real etymological meaning
of the word, the new birth, foretold its
fate; Rome had been born again; it had
flourished with its dependence on remote
ideals; it had become the property of
scholars; it had made a schism between the
real life of people and their way of appear-
ing in literature, — exactly the same difference as there is in English between the
Latin and what we are accustomed to call
the Anglo-Saxon words of our vocabulary;
and, after it had tamed and civilized men
for two hundred and fifty years, we saw
the result at the end of the last century, in

the aversion to confusion, enthusiasm, and everything inexplicable. On one side stood life, with all its charm; there was no confusion, — the understanding appeared to have settled everything. To be sure, there were suffering, ignorance, misery; but for the lucky ones who had won the prizes in the lottery there was no unpleasant feeling of duty to disturb their enjoyment. On the other side were fanatics, enthusiasts, discontented with the current neat solution of the universe, who indulged in obviously foolish longings and refused to listen to the voice of reason; yet, after all, the grumbler is the man of the future, though odious in the present.

All of this polished materialism Wieland expressed very neatly, as it was expressed by Voltaire and by hosts of forgotten writers in France and by a certain number in England, whose ears were too deaf to hear the premonitory mutterings of change. They broke away from pedantry and, as it were, walked on their own legs without the aid of crutches; they abandoned all prejudices, and took men as they found them; they had the art of saying things gracefully: it was only the men who were full of the future who stammered and bungled. Sterne, in England, represents the unpedantic writers of the new time, who had acquired a Gallic grace, and, with the grace, some of the Gallic frivolity. Wieland, too, showed how even Germans could give lessons in worldly wisdom, and his fame was at once made.

To understand just what that civilization meant is not perfectly simple; but Wieland throws a light upon it. Like most writers, he cannot be exactly defined by even the most careful adjectives of praise or blame. Censure or approbation are equally far from expressing his importance and from conveying a clear notion of the precise place that he occupied. The mere shifting of popular taste, with regard to his work, will make this statement clear. In the last century we should have heard nothing but rapturous admiration; and it is not merely a difference in presidents that makes it unlikely that any one now holding that office should again translate his "Oberon," as John Quincy Adams did. The difference is in ourselves, and in the progress of literature, which has absorbed many influences besides the one Wieland represented, and cannot linger by his contribution to the total work. Whether we like it or not, his work is there, and it is deserving of consideration. This will show us that a good part of Wieland's service to letters lay in breaking ground for freedom in art. We saw how Brockes expressed the new found delight in nature, with what keen joy he expressed his rapture over the delicate whiteness of the new cherry blossoms; and to many, doubtless, his exultation appeared like most complete triviality; yet he was uttering a new truth, that the world was in itself beautiful, and that the eye of man was

capable of other pleasures than reading
about the chess-play of various intellectual
interests. When we remember, however,
that his enjoyment of this innocent specta-
cle only led him up to amazement at the
undoubted superiority of celestial joys, we
shall see that he was poisoned by the moral
bias, like all of us moderns, who are in-
capable of enjoying beauty without pond-
ering on the associations, chiefly of a
didactic kind, that it may call up within us.
Every new aspect had to be recommended
as a moral teacher. We still know the
necessity of this; we are still aware that a
thing which is beautiful has to be excused
or apologized for, or palliated, — shuffled
in, after some fashion, as good for our
morals. Our insistance on this secondary
end is the reason why men who wish to be
honest so often take great pains to be im-
moral. They are disgusted with our insin-
cerity, and exaggerate the grim horror of
the truth.

What Wieland did was to attempt part of the general regeneration of man from the burthen of authority. Brockes peeped at the truth; Wieland expressed it ripened and enlarged. Brockes, we remember, sang of the comfort of stretching in bed; Wieland tried to point out how man was not a merely intellectual creature, but that every emotion of which he was capable was required for the perfect man. He detested the dreamy vagueness of his contemporaries, and had a clearly-defined intellectual perception that beauty had been expelled by teaching; and he found no delight in seeking for it in the fantastic shapes of the clouds; he called for concrete enjoyment. It was the narrowness of his ideal that injured him. The material philosophy of " let us eat, drink, and be merry," overlooks the remorse and regret of satiety which goes to the debit account, and has to be considered by one who is at all wise; yet it has done good work by advancing the claims of one side of long-starved human nature, — a complex thing, — and thus contributing to the general discussion of how man shall grow, the fact that it is not by the intellect alone, or by the emotions alone; while these two elements take good care to prove that it is not by material pleasures alone. A number of complicated influences fed the romantic revival, which was really an assertion of man's individuality; and it is only gradually that we are learning that they are found in every human being, and not in imaginary heroes alone.

Wieland had detractors and rivals. The literary currents were growing complicated as they were in England; the old and new were meeting and producing strange results. Two of these were important enough to demand a few words. Gessner (1730–87) was the first writer of German, of modern times, who received the honours of translation into all the European languages. He looked at nature as he had been taught to do by Brockes and by Thomson, and he drew little idyllic pictures, in which we nowadays notice especially the frame and the composition rather than the vivid representations of nature. Yet, in comparison with the avowedly ideal persons in the old Arcadian romances, these Greuze-like figures were genuine, and their sentimentality only added to their likeness to the life about them. The Arcadians were a long-lived race; when the interest of readers lay in the direction of lofty virtues, the romances reflected this; now, when arose the love of nature, though of nature seen through streaming eyes, Gessner catered to it, and gave in a complete and finished form what was crude in the translation and imitation of Ossian, in whom the more modern feeling of nature was soon to find expression.

In Gleim's military songs we find another division of the new spirit seeking utterance. They were patriotic outbursts, inspired by the success of Frederick the Great. It is more as an indication of the new change in men's hopes and interests, than from any enormous poetic value, that these poems are important. The country was awakening from the political apathy that kept literature a thing apart from life and a matter of formal interest. Real feeling of civil life was showing itself after a long absence; and patriotism, which had fed itself on the romantic antiquity of a really unknown past, now had real life set before it.

Another important contribution came from the *Volkslieder*, which may be best studied in the simple record of the Göttinger "Hainbund;" although, since every chronological division is an incomplete one, it carries us down almost further than we have a right to be at this stage of our consideration of the subject. Yet the outburst which we are about to study occupies an intermediate place between the raw antiquity which Klopstock furthered and the later study of mediæval history, which in many forms became one of the most important decisions of the Romantic revival. Inasmuch as it was at this time crude, it may fairly be examined now, when our attention is turned to what was the budding season of the enthusiasm that was soon to burst out into full flower. Certainly it is not hard to perceive qualities that are generally associated with the name of Germany, in what we find in these letters of the year 1772. Voss, for example, writes thus to Brückner: —

You ought to have been here on the 12th of September! The two Millers, Hahn, Hölty, Wehrs, and I went in the evening to a neighbouring village. The moon was full. We gave ourselves up to the unrestrained enjoyment of the beauties of nature. We drank milk in a peasant's hut, and then walked out into the open fields. Here we found a little oak-grove; and it at once occurred to us all to swear friendship beneath these sacred trees. We set wreaths of oak-leaves around our hats, seized one another's hands, danced about the narrow space, called to the moon and stars to be witnesses of our union, and

vowed eternal friendship. Then we bound ourselves
to the most complete uprightness in our judgments of
one another, and, for this object in view, to celebrate
our usual meetings with more exactness and greater
ceremony. Every one of us is to write a poem on
that evening, and we are to renew the ceremony every
year.

October 26, he writes: —

A few days before his departure, Ewald invited the
whole of our Parnassus and Bürger to a farewell ban-
quet. That was a real assemblage of poets, and we
all revelled like Anacreon and Horace; Boie, our
Werdomar, at the head in an arm-chair; on both
sides of the table the younger bards adorned with
oak-leaves. Healths were drunk. First Klopstock's!
Boie took his glass, rose, and shouted, "Klopstock!"
Every one did the same, uttered the great name, and,
after a solemn silence, drank. Then Ramler's! Not
quite so solemnly. Lessing's, Gleim's, Gessner's, Ger- ·
stenberg's, Uz's, Weisse's, etc., then my Brückner,
with his Doris. A holy shudder must have seized
them when the whole choir, — Hahn, and the Millers,
with manly German throats; Boie and Bürger, with
their silver voices, and the rest of us, — shouted the
fiery "Lebe." Bürger called "Wieland! Down with
Voltaire," etc. Next you were solemnly chosen a
member. The oath to further religion, virtue, sensibility, and pure, innocent wit, will not cost you much
trouble; and the object of our society — to aid one
another by mutual criticism — you can assist by letter;

for we communicate with one another by letter, in order to secure greater freedom.

One or two additional quotations will dispel any lingering doubts with regard to their abundant enthusiasm. Klopstock's birthday was thus celebrated, July 2, 1773:

Immediately after dinner we assembled in Hahn's room. A long table was set and adorned with flowers. At the head was an empty arm-chair covered with roses and gilliflowers, and on it were Klopstock's complete works. Under the chair lay Wieland's "Idris" torn into fragments. First, Hahn read a few of Klopstock's odes that referred to Germany; then we drank coffee. Our pipe-lighters were made out of Wieland's works. Boie, who does not smoke, had to light one, and stamp on the fragments of the "Idris." Then we drank in Rhine wine Klopstock's health, Luther's memory, Hermann's, the health of the "Bund;" then Ebert's, Goethe's (don't you know him yet?), Herder's, etc. Then the talk grew. We talked about freedom, with our hats on our heads, about Germany, virtue,—and you can imagine how we talked! Then we ate, drank punch, and at last we burned Wieland's "Idris" and his likeness.

This is the last: —

September 12 will often cost me tears. It was the day of parting from the Counts Stolberg and their excellent chamberlain Clauswitz. The afternoon and evening were tolerably cheerful, though at times a trifle quieter than usual. In some we detected secret tears of the heart. These are the bitterest, Ernestina,—bitterer than those which bedew the cheek. The young Count's face was terrible; he strove to be cheerful, and every expression was melancholy. . . . (*Evening*, 10 *o'clock*). — I was forced to play on the piano. Perhaps the music gave the others some alleviation; but in me, who had to experience every melting effect in order to render it again, it inflicted only deeper wounds. It was midnight before the Stolbergs arrived. But who can describe the three terrible hours we passed together in the night! Every one wanted to cheer up the others, and hence arose a confusion of grief and simulated joy which was like madness. We had punch made, for the night was cold. We tried to dispel our gloom by singing, and chose Miller's "Abschiedslied." Here all pretence was vain. Our tears welled forth; our voices gradually failed us. We asked the same questions ten times over; we swore eternal friendship; we embraced; we sent messages to Klopstock. Then it struck three. We could no longer restrain our agony; we tried to make ourselves more wretched, and sang the "Abschiedslied" once more, and sang it to the end with difficulty. We were all weeping aloud. After a fearful pause, Clauswitz arose, "Now, my children, the time has come!" I flew to him, and I do not know what I did. Miller drew the Count to the window and showed him a star. I can't go on, dear Ernestina; my tears are falling anew. When Clauswitz let me go, the Counts were off. It was the most terrible night I ever knew.

CHAPTER V.

SURELY letters like these enable one to understand the mood in which "Werther" was written and read; but they take us away from the consideration of some of the earlier incidents. Lessing, whose health was drunk by these zealous revellers, has been left till now, in order that the total impression of his fine character and momentous impulse might appear in one distinct whole. We shall see that he includes much that lies dim in his contemporaries, and also that he, like every one else, was a man of his time. This must be distinctly borne in mind, not to the discredit of Lessing, but as a simple historic fact. That quality which we call genius it may at present be out of our power to define. Yet the direction in which this genius shall find expression, the errors which it shall sweep away, as well as those which it may accept, the language which it shall use, are as inevitable and as capable of explanation as the linguistic or grammatical peculiarities which shall mark a writer's style. Just as an author must use the existing vocabulary, he must correct or express existing errors; and he is bound by the limitations of humanity as to the extent to which he may be able to advance beyond the starting-place. What he does is to say what his contemporaries feel, rising above them, but in the direction in which they are moving. So much, at least, we are justified in saying of Lessing; and it perhaps deserves saying about him, because sometimes his countrymen have spoken of him as a man who accomplished all that he did by sheer intellectual force, without any relation to his contemporaries.

If we trace the course of Lessing's life

and action, we shall see that he started with his generation, and that what is wonderful in him is the way in which he answered the questions that naturally arose as literature was growing. This was the difference between him and other men, that he answered the questions that arose, instead of contenting himself with the obsolete solutions that satisfied his contemporaries. He was born in 1729; and, after a busy boyhood and youth, in which he equipped himself very well for the discussion of many subjects, he began his literary career at a very early age. We have seen that Gottsched, who was then at the height of his influence, was working heartily in the direction of improving the German stage; and Lessing soon tried his hand at writing plays. This was far from being the only employment of his busy pen. He not only composed poems, but he criticised the work of most of his contemporaries; and there was scarcely a single department of thought

in which he did not interest himself.[1]
What first strikes the eye in running over
his work is its fragmentary state. Lessing
and Herder, the two men who raised German literature from provincialism to prominence, and, one may almost say without
exaggeration, established the lines on which
it was to move, have this quality in common, that their work is in a fragmentary
condition. The impulse that Herder gave
to Germany, and through Germany to the
civilized world, — for by his time that country filled its own boundaries, and every

[1] In their interesting books on German literature, both
Hinrichs and Grucker lay a great deal of weight on the
fact that the literature of Germany is built up on critical
work. This is true; but yet it is well to remember that
the large amount of criticism in that country is merely a
sign of widespread interest in literature, and that elsewhere
copious discussion accompanies creative work. Dryden,
for example, was always writing about the proper way to
write. Wordsworth and Coleridge defended the position
they and their contemporaries took in their poems; and in
France, about 1830, the critical warfare was quite as important as the literature it illustrated and advocated.
Everywhere and at all times people will talk about subjects
that interest them. This condition is far from being peculiar to Germany.

impulse that it received affected its neigh-
bours, — was due, not to formal books, with
a beginning, a middle, and an end, but
to remarks dropped here and there, that
were not formal developments of definite
problems, but happy statements of novel
truths. These fell on rich ground, and in-
fluenced every man, just as Bible texts
console the pious, who do not weave them
into an intricate system of theology. The
fragmentariness of what he said and of
what Lessing said does not appear to stand
in their way. After all, stammering is not
a quality to be acquired with pains; but it
is better to stammer out the truth than to
utter glibly empty platitudes; and when we
are reminded, of this or that writer, that his
work represents no system, it may be fair
to pause a moment before being overwhelmed, and to ask what in the past is
the relative value of the men with systems,
and of the men who were wise enough to
see that a system of the universe was but

another attempt to square the circle. Socrates is regarded as a man who helped the intellectual growth of the world; but the Socratic system is not yet known. Montaigne has some reputation as a thinker. Where was his system? Old temples are not the only things that time overthrows; and of Plato — of every man who aims at the solution of every question — we have left much dust, and a greater or smaller collection of fragments that alone move the world. Let us, then, not mourn that Lessing's swift intelligence made the selection of what should be given to the world; and if for Lessing we read Emerson, the remark still holds good.

In Lessing's case the fragmentariness is sufficiently explained by the number of his interests and his delight in controversy.

The fables which his contemporaries were writing, with a complacent belief that they were filling every requisition that could be made, Lessing also wrote. His restless energy inspired him to attempt a serious discussion of the nature of the fable, in which he set some of Breitinger's false notions right, but did not fairly come to a ripe conclusion. Then, too, he wrote odes, epigrams, and indeed all the accustomed little poems of the day, and with such success that he acquired some reputation in foreign parts; but no one knew better than himself how far he was from being a real poet. His own lack of poetic capacity he was never tired of confessing. Although he wrote three plays that were the first in Germany to deserve a place in literature, — a place they still hold, — he maintained that he was no dramatist. He knew, what posterity has agreed in acknowledging, that his main merit was as a critic. It is of the utmost importance to know Lessing's plays, but it is a great mistake to rest contented with that knowledge, and not to study his critical writing. To be sure, much of this has become old-fashioned; many of the points

which he took up are now permanently
settled; some have at this day only a historic interest; but everything that Lessing
wrote impresses on our minds the vision of
an indefatigable lover of truth, who refused
to take commonplaces for granted, and was
the deadly foe of pedantry and convention.
These were always his animating principles,
and in the drama, in general literature, in
archæology and theology, he cleared the
ground as no other one man has ever done
in the history of any country.

Let us examine what he did with the
drama by way of precept and example. In
Gottsched's hands the stage was turned
wholly in the direction of the lifeless imitation of French models. The same formal
exactness in England flourished in Addison's " Cato," and lingered until Johnson's
" Irene." Its final expulsion from that
country we may place in 1756, the date of
his preface to Shakespeare. But before
Johnson wrote that famous preface, the

unities, which had been exotics . at the best, had withered and fallen after bearing but a few fruits, as juiceless as hot-house oranges. In France, too, the change was taking place in the dramatic literature under the leadership of Diderot. Lessing in Germany fought the same fight. Since it was the same question, the conflict between what was reputed to be the classic stage and what is commonly called the romantic, that was agitating these three countries simultaneously, it may perhaps be worth our while to examine the way in which independence was sought in each one of them. In fact, not only is this the most interesting way of regarding the subject, but it is distinctly the most accurate, for it is impossible to understand what Diderot and Lessing did without knowing the English stage; and, more than this, inasmuch as waves of thought know geographical boundaries as little as the waves of the sea know their geographical names, the contests that were waged in these separate countries were all parts of one great battle, not yet wholly finished, between the old and the new — between the Renaissance and romanticism. Just as in a real battle, the soldier in a cornfield does not know very clearly what is going on behind a neighbouring hill, although the victory of the line at that point weakens the enemy in his front, so this fight was fought with each contestant seeing most clearly the enemy directly in his face. Now, however, we can view the whole battle as it raged for something like a century, and its importance gives greater glory to Lessing, who was the ablest general officer in the field.

The classic drama first fixed itself in France, deriving its principles from Italy, and taking the place of the crude drama of impossibilities which was represented by Hardy. In France it found its natural home, and from there it spread to England and Germany. In England the French influence was slow in its conquest of modern taste. The Puritans, by closing the play-houses in 1642, had broken with the past, but the early inspiration was already fairly dead. With the Restoration and the revival of Beaumont and Fletcher, as well as in the work of the new writers who had not forgotten the old traditions, we see the native aversion to rules holding out for a long time against accepting many shackles at once. Dryden's indecision about the relative merits of blank verse and poetry; his comments — as in the famous "Essay of Dramatic Poesy" — on the French stage; and, more than anything else, the general crudity of the English heroic drama, with its excesses and extravagances, show how far the English play-writers were from imitating the French. The stream that started in the classic French drama met another and a very turbid stream, that refused to flow in bounds until Addison, who had already

laughed at the heroic plays, let his " Cato "
be acted, and gave the authority of his
name to the most rigid formality.   Yet
even his adherence to these rules, at the
very time — it is curious to notice — when he
was defending Milton and beginning the
war against similar artificiality in epic
poetry, inspired but few imitators.   Rowe
had already, in a crude way, gone back to
Shakespeare, and a few years later Lillo, in
his " George Barnwell," had shown that a
tragedy did not demand social position in
its main characters.   Richardson and Lillo
established the sway of the family novel and
the domestic tragedy, and their effect was
even greater on the continent than in England, where there has always existed
marked intolerance for the discussion of
general principles.   Moreover, in England
the classic plays had too slight a hold to
need much exorcising.   They vanished
almost before they had become firmly
established.   In France, however, they were

part of the apparent constitution of the
universe, and the attack upon them required
a campaign of nearly a century before victory was won. La Motte, a writer of no
great merit, opened the battle with an attack
on the writers, pointing out that the unity
of place made it necessary to lug people
into strange places, whither they would not
have gone naturally, and asking whether
the spectators, who knew that they were in
the theatre, could not as easily imagine
themselves in Athens as in Rome in the
course of a single play, and showing that in
the opera the variety of place caused no
confusion.[1] He attacked the unity of time

---

[1] To show how the unity of place did not destroy freedom, the Abbé d'Aubignac, in his "Pratique du Théâtre"
(Amsterdam: 1725), i. 90, says: — "On pourroit feindre
au palais sur le bord de la mer abandonné à de pauvres
gens de la compagne; un prince arrivant aux côtes par
naufrage, qui le feroit orner de riches tapisseries, lustres,
bras dorez, tableaux, et autres meubles précieux. Après
on y feroit mettre en feu par quelque avanture, et le faisant
tomber dans l'embrasement, la mer paroîtroit derrière sur
laquelle on pourroit encore representer un combat de vais-
seaux. Si bien que dans cinq changements de Théâtre
l'unité de lieu seroit ingénieusement gardée."

with the same useless weapon, good sense, but with the result that sensible people will expect, — he became an object of ridicule. Voltaire, especially, turned on him with violence, saying: — "The spectator is but three hours at the play, consequently the acting must last only three hours. Cinna, Andromaque, Bajazet last no longer. If a few other pieces demand more time, this is a license which is only pardonable in view of the beauty of the work; and the greater the license, the greater the fault." Marmontel, too, frequently advocated a change. La Motte recommended tragedies in prose. Lachaussée wrote plays in prose about people in common life; the seed took root, and change was in the air.

Among the inspiring causes, besides the influence of the English stage[1] and natural distaste for the dwindling glories

[1] The Théâtre Anglais (8 vols.) appeared between 1745 and 1749. The first four volumes were almost entirely devoted to Shakespeare.

of the classic drama, we may count the new influence of the novel, which, by accustoming the reader to frequent change of scene, helped to destroy the rigidity of the unity of place, and left on the reader an impression of the advantage of prose for the expression of thought. It also showed the value of the unconventional hero. The spectator became more aware than formerly of the chains which the dramatist had to assume. This was all part of the general disintegration of authority which had gone to the making of the etiquette of literature that marked the establishment of pseudo-classicism. There independence was opposed, as independence in manners is always opposed; the authorities felt averse to anyone who had his own views of literature, as one feels now about those who do not comply with convention, but have manners of their own. The same liberality extended itself, also, to the tolerance of translations and imitations. At the time of which we are now speaking, independence was beginning to assert itself, and it began with asking for freedom of the emotions.

The most important defender of the new spirit was Diderot, who wrote much about the stage, urging the player to watch nature, and in his "Paradox" affirming that extreme sensibility makes mediocre actors; mediocre sensibility, bad actors; and that an absolute lack of sensibility makes actors really sublime. He condemned excessive gesture and emphasis, and praised realistic scenery. The best plays, he said, were those that combined tragedy and comedy, and he tried his hand at composing plays for a model to his disciples. What injured both his precepts and his practice was his insistence on the need of moral teaching. "It is always virtue and virtuous people that a man should have in view when writing. Oh, what a gain it would be for mankind if all the imitative arts should pro-

pose one common object, and were to com-
bine with the laws in making us love virtue
and hate vice!" This was an old error that
was especially prominent in the last century. We shall come across it in Lessing,
just as we find it in the earliest writers on
the subject.[1]

What especially distinguishes Lessing's
work about the stage is this, that he fought
almost single-handed, while in England the
change of the drama towards simplicity was
but one part of a general effort to abandon
an artificial system; and in France the
movement was furthered by a number of
fellow - workers. The condition of the
theatre in Germany when Lessing began to
write was most lamentable, and those who
were supplying it with material were slav-

---

[1] D'Aubignac, *Op. cit.* i. 5: — "La principale règle du
poëme dramatique est que les vertus y soient toûjours
recompensées ou pour le moins y soient toûjours louées,
malgré les outrages de la Fortune et que les vices y soient
toûjours punis ou pour le moins toûjours en horreur quand
même ils y triomphent."

ishly devoted to the utmost rigor of the French rules. They had no admirable past to which they could look back; for the mediæval glory of Germany was remoter than the civilization of Rome. The popular theatre was a mass of vulgarities, that represented only the degradation of the populace; and the absence of national life deprived the Germans of what has always been the strongest inspiration of a real drama. Yet, narrow as the field was, it was one that held out the most temptations to young writers. The more they tried, however, the more evident it became that the French taste, which was the natural expression of that nation, was an exotic in the less civilized Germany. The imported elegance had no roots in the nation, and it even failed to satisfy those who, like Frederick the Great, preferred to get the French flavour in the French tongue. We have seen that Klopstock led his generation back to a remote and romantic nationalism. It was Lessing's glory that he brought the drama into close and actual relations with human life. This he accomplished in two ways — by criticism and by his own original work. From the beginning, Lessing's criticism of Gottsched was unsparing. What was ridiculous in that would-be dictator he lost no chance to ridicule; and this he did without entering the camp of the Swiss school. Yet he began with the intention, not of overthrowing everything that the example of the French taught, but of widening its narrow limits. He wrote the beginnings of many plays, but it was with the "Miss Sara Sampson" (1755) that he first appeared as a dramatic writer of any importance. His earlier work is only lit up by the brilliancy of what he now began to do. Of itself it was of the nature of school exercises. Already Lessing had studied the discussion that was going on in France and England about the stage, and in the very title of this play we see its descent from the English domestic drama. This fact, that it owed its origin to the literature of another country, is but one of the many instances of the futility of looking anywhere for that form of originality which to the student is as incomprehensible as a sixth sense. There is a vague notion that the mysterious thing called genius is capable of evoking something out of nothing by direct exercise of creative power. While this idea has vanished from science, it still survives in those departments of human activity which have not yet come fully under scientific treatment, and poets and painters enjoy in the popular estimation a privilege which has been denied to nature. For one thing, the fact that the Greek and Roman classics came down to us only in fragments—and these the best—confirmed those who studied only those two literatures in the belief that the great works of the Greeks were the result of a sort of lucky chance, and that the Romans, when they wanted a tragedy, or comedy, or epic, set a safe fashion by sitting down and copying their predecessors. They had no better opportunity to observe the growth of literature than has the hasty traveller who studies the history of painting in the Tribune of the Uffizi, in which the masterpieces are crowded together, and the splendor of human achievement strikes the dazed and delighted spectator without the intrusion of any reminder of the toil by which it was attained, or of the forgotten failures that make it clear that not for us alone is success rare and difficult. In Greek literature, especially, we have only the mountain-peaks, and not the expanse of plain, so that we cannot draw the man with all the fulness that is possible when we have to do with modern countries. And, too, just as Darwin would never have hit upon his theory of evolution if the fauna he had seen had consisted of nothing but horses, cows, elephants, and dogs, so it would have

been with the students of the classics. It was
the blending lines of the pigeons that first
led him to observe the interchangeability of
species; and with all the evidence at our
command in modern literature, we detect
the wonderful connection between the writings of different countries. The growth of
the *bourgeoisie* in England was the inspiring
cause of the family novel and the domestic
drama. This advance in civilization spread
to other countries, and with the same results.
The English and German imitations of the
"Spectator" carried the new feeling, which
was furthered by the study of nature; and
to the eye of science there is no material
difference between a king and a peasant —
or at least since all discoveries are gradual
—between a king and a respectable citizen.
Love of the peasant was still a sentimental
weakness, and, we may say, yet awaits the
time when the peasant shall discover his
own importance. The exaggerated insistence on purely national traits was not a

fault of Lessing's, who was too truly a man of the eighteenth century not to perceive that civilization was a single task in which all European nations were allies. They all spoke one language, though in different dialects. Later, the feeling of national differences was intensified by abhorrence of the superficiality of cosmopolitanism, and, distinctly, by the struggle for life against the French; but now we are learning once more the great lesson that we are all one family. When science has made this clear, we shall see that the leaven has again been working in literature, and meanwhile even a hasty examination will show that there is free trade — in thought at least — throughout the civilized world.

The change from a drama that represented only kings and heroes of princely birth to one that concerned itself with human beings, was as inevitable a thing as is the change in government from despotism to democracy, with the growth of the im-

portance of the individual. There is a certain monotony in civilization which may be
exemplified in a thousand ways. The large
gas-pipes, for instance, that are laid in every
street, and have the smaller branches running into every house, which again feed the
ramifying tubes that supply the single lights,
may remind one of the advance from the
general to the particular which characterizes every form of human thought. The
classical tragedies presented a few acknowledged truths vividly and strongly. Their
simplicity and universality were of great
service in inculcating a few general principles, and no one can easily overestimate
the educational value of a code that repe-
tition made familiar to every student. The
mere mention of Cæsar's name brought with
it a picture of ambition. Scipio stood for
self-control; Medea for the stricken mother.
Lucretia became the incarnation of matronly
honour; Virginia, that of maidenly purity.
Europe was civilized by the experience of

other races, and the study of the classics was a labor-saving device which deserves all the credit that is not a mere echo of what people imagine that they ought to say to show their cultivation. But in the last century the time began to appear when authority ceased to serve its long-lived purpose as an educational means. What the classics — and especially the Latin classics — could teach had been thoroughly learned. We know that now it would be difficult to oppose a tyrant by calling him Tarquin, and we have as dim a feeling for the Roman proper names as we have after a bountiful dinner on the twenty-second of December for the sufferings of the Pilgrim fathers. What Rome could do for the world had been assimilated, — to eradicate it would have been barbarous; — but to go on repeating it as if it contained the whole truth that man could attain to would have been intellectual bondage. Consequently men simply left it on one side and took another path.

There were several inviting them. The populace had already found pleasure in the contemplation of itself and of very unclassical heroes, and the habit spread. Moreover, with democracy in the air, what were kings but convenient formulas? Not in vain, as Boswell's father told Dr. Johnson, did Cromwell "gar kings ken that they had a lith in their necks;" and when kings could be robbed of their influence, to say nothing of their lives, by their people, it became evident that those who held the power were also objects of interest. The lessons they had to learn were not the vague truths that Rome could teach, but the application of these truths to modern conditions.

Let us also notice, here, that the new lessons were taught with an outburst of sentiment. Just as the present new treatment of the poor, by the rigid application of scientific rules, was preceded by the gushing period when charity consisted in putting one's hands into one's pockets and bringing out gold pieces that — not unnaturally — made the pauper happy, the development of modern literature without classic crutches began with copious floods of tears, as if those authors foresaw the melancholy consequences of the new responsibilities that the world was assuming.

Then, too, it is not with impunity that man is born when certain influences are at work; these he cannot escape any more than he can escape fashions in hats. Lillo's " George Barnwell " was a king done small. The tragedy was like an old tragedy, with a clerk's stool instead of a throne, and a quill-pen in the place of a sceptre. What would have been regal was made civic. For the overweening crimes of a king, Lillo put a London apprentice succumbing to gross temptations; this was the value of the change, that it was made clear that a change was possible; its development awaited time. For the discovery that freedom is desirable is very remote from the

discovery of the best way in which to secure and maintain freedom.

In writing this "Miss Sara Sampson,"
Lessing took the only step that was possible for a man abreast with his time. The
significance of the school can hardly be
overestimated, although this bears but a remote relation to its æsthetic value. What
was gained by the introduction of human
beings who, so to speak, wore no halo, ran
a great risk of being lost by the substitution of more conventional and social punishments for the more serious, because eternal,
ethical punishments of the older tragedy.
The gallows that adorned the last scene of
"George Barnwell" was a feeble substitute
for more genuine tragic horror, and by the
introduction of the horrid vengeance of the
ministers of law, by having fate personified
as a police officer, we see the door opened
for the melodrama, and the same unnecessary error that the modern French novelists
make, when, in their effort to write about

common people, they pick out uncommonly
bad ones.   I call the error unnecessary, and
so it is when judged after the event, but,
historically, it is necessary or at least uniformly true that we find simplicity the last
thing attained.   The whole gradual lesson
of life is the reduction of emphasis.   Lessing speedily learned this truth which was
enforced upon him by his eighteenth century
training, and in his "Minna von Barnhelm"
(1763) we find it controlling and directing
him, for it is never to be forgotten that Lessing belonged to the eighteenth century.
This is not merely a statement of historical
fact, but an explanation of his merits and
of his limitations.   We shall find abundant instances to prove the assertion in
his critical writings, as well as in his original writings, which are always of the nature
of illustrations of the theoretical position
he attained by dint of intellectual work.
Thus "Miss Sara Sampson" is like a lec-
turer's drawing on the black-board, wherein

Lessing makes plain what he has to say
about the domestic drama; and in " Minna
von Barnhelm " we find a play that throws
light upon his late theories about the stage.
What first strikes us is its literary perfection, and this is a quality that marks the
work of many writers of the latter part of
the last century, who were keenly sensitive
to the thoughts that inspired that interesting period, but whose eyes were not dazzled,
and whose hands were not made uncertain,
by the contemplation of the whole mighty
upheaval of the romantic revival. They
preserved a concinnity which was lost with
the good manners that existed before the
French revolution. Voltaire's French, for
instance, has known no later followers,
though it was used more or less well by
many of his contemporaries, and in English
literature we see something similar in Goldsmith's " Vicar of Wakefield," which was
the last book written in that language that
can be read and admired by both scholars

and ignorant people. Lessing and Goldsmith both employed a tool that had become
flexible and easy by long practice. Even
Klopstock, although old errors clung to
him, as Dantzel well points out, in trying
to make a literal substitution of the Scan-
dinavian for the Græco-Roman mythology,
and in forging new fetters after the old
fashion,[1] opened wide fields to the imagin-
ation, to do justice to which exceeded his
own powers. Lessing, on the other hand,
was controlled by the more rigid and narrower limits of the vanishing generation;
although the two men were contemporaries,
Klopstock belonged to the younger race.
In the second place, we notice that in
"Minna von Barnhelm," Lessing succeeded
in producing a play that drew its strength
from the fact that it was a vivid picture
of German life. A chord was touched that
had been silent for centuries; the Germans
had imitated the French with heavy-handed

[1] See his "Lessing," i, 493.

levity, they had tried to sing as Horace sang, and to praise the juice of the grape as Anacreon was supposed to have done; but now German life found its poet, and that country at once was fitted to take its proper place among the nations of Europe. The play was one result of the Seven Years' War, which had already called Gleim away from the production of Anacreontic frivolities to singing patriotic songs. Frederick the Great, to be sure, did not care for German literature; a taste for poetry, as Kuno Fischer has truly said,[1] is something that is formed in youth, a remark that is especially true of busy men, and in his youth Gottsched was the prophet of French taste. The German writers were never tired of making allusions to Frederick's indifference to their work. Not only was it impossible to recall the golden age of Latin literature without thinking of Augustus, but the position of

[1] See his " Lessing als Reformator der deutschen Sprache." 1ten Theil, p. 83.

Richelieu and of Louis XIV. in France towards writers aroused envy in every German who was interested in letters. When
Frederick, a few days before Rossbach
(1757), gave an audience to Gottsched, the
writer said Germany lacked an Augustus,
Frederick retorted that they had one. "'But
no Mæcenas,' I answered." [It is Gottsched
who describes the scene.] "'There you are
right,' said the king. When I urged further that German writers were discouraged
because the nobility and the courtiers were
too familiar with French and too ignorant
of German to understand and appreciate
their own language, he said, 'That is true,
for I have never read a German book since
I was a boy, and I speak the language like
a coachman' [they were talking in French]
'but now I'm an old fellow of forty-six and
have no time to give to it.'" Three years
later, in talking with Gellert, Frederick
asked, "Why have we no more good authors?"—a tactful question, it will be

noticed. "Your majesty has formed a prejudice against the Germans." "No, I can't
say that." "At least, against German writers." "That is true." "A good many reasons might be assigned why the Germans
have not produced very much first-rate
work. While the arts and sciences flourished among the Greeks, the Romans were
at war. Possibly the present is our war-
making age; possibly the Germans have not
had an Augustus." "What! Do you want
an Augustus for all Germany?" "Not exactly that; I only wish that each monarch
should encourage the geniuses in his own
territory." Here the king changed the subject, for that is a privilege which kings
enjoy in conversation with private citizens.

When, a few years after Lessing's death,
Mirabeau brought forward the same accusation against the king, Frederick replied,
"You don't know what you are talking
about. Just because I have left my subjects
free play and have seemed to take no inter-

est in their writings, I have done more for them and for enlightenment than if I had tried to drive them." But if it is possible now to be grateful 'that Frederick did not drill the Prussians in literature, it is easy to see that by his genius and bravery he gave the state that independence of outside control, and that feeling of self-existence, which animated Lessing at least in writing "Minna von Barnhelm." The story of his life brings out very clearly the increasing struggle he had with fate, owing to the indifference of patrons of literature, but Frederick's great deeds made the play possible.

And how delightful the play is! Tellheim, the hero, is a wounded officer who has been fighting bravely under Frederick, and is now discharged; but before he can receive his papers he must make clear an apparent discrepancy in his accounts. It seems that, being obliged to levy a contribution from a region in which he had been quartered, out of commiseration for the general suffering which the war had caused, he had contributed the sum of two thousand pistoles out of his own pocket. When the peace was signed, he charged the amount as part of the war debt. The note given by the district was recognized to be genuine, but it was regarded as a bribe to Tellheim for reducing the enforced contribution to its minimum; and, until the matter is examined, he is forbidden to leave the town. Meanwhile he has spent all his own money; most of his servants have run away, carrying with them his belongings; one, Just, by name, is left him. His sergeant-major, Werner, who twice saved his life in the war, is living near by, on a little estate that he owns. In these circumstances he awaits his fate, — poor, wounded, suspected of dishonesty, and further saddened by the necessity of breaking his engagement. He had been betrothed to Minna von Barnhelm, who was filled with admiration for his generosity to the people from whom he had been ordered to extort a levy. But after a while he had ceased to answer her letters, and she had determined to seek him. In the company of her maid, Franziska, and of her uncle, Count Bruchsall, a Saxon nobleman, who detested the Germans, and had lived in Italy while the war was going on, she reached Berlin while her uncle was detained at the next station. By chance she goes to the inn where Tellheim was staying,—the "King of Spain." She is rich, Tellheim is poor; so during his absence the landlord, without ado, dispossesses him of his comfortable quarters, thrusts his belongings into a wretched hole in the garret, telling Minna that the officer had voluntarily offered her his room. Tellheim, in his wrath, determines to leave the inn at once, and, having no ready money for the payment of his bill, gives Just his engagement ring to pawn. Just gives it to the landlord, who shows it to Minna, and thus she learns that Tellheim is here. She thus gets a view of the whole matter; but she knows the man, and perceives that her difficulties have only begun. He is as proud as Lucifer, and his pride is the only thing he will not sacrifice for anyone. He can never bring himself to owe his relief to her, and all her assurances that she would gladly share his misery she knows would be idle. But she sees her way; as a rich heiress she has no chance; she knows that if she pretends to reject him because she is too poor and miserable, the obstinate creature will be melted; and so it happens. The innocent deception is finally exposed, and the curtain falls on the best German comedy that perhaps was ever written.

The ingenuity of the plot is really secondary to the skill with which the characters display themselves. The ingenuity with which Tellheim is drawn is above all praise. In the first place, the enthusiasm that Just feels for him prepares us for making his acquaintance with a prejudice in his favor.

His sergeant-major has just brought him five hundred thalers, but he refuses to touch them, and yet he is so poor that he bids his servant make out the amount due him. Then comes in the widow of one of his old fellow-soldiers, to whom Tellheim had lent four hundred thalers, and who, on his death-bed, had enjoined upon her that she must pay them. She had sold everything to raise the money, which she now brings.

"Let me count the money," she says. "No, indeed; Marloff in debt to me? That can hardly be. Let me see" (he examines his note-book); "I don't find anything about it."

"You must have mislaid his note, but that formality makes no difference. Allow me."

"No, madam, I never mislay anything of the kind. If I have not it, that is a sign that I have never had it, or that it was paid and I gave it back to him."

"Major!"

"Certainly, madam; Marloff owed me

nothing. I can't remember that he was ever in my debt. Indeed, it is more likely that he was my creditor. I have never managed to pay everything I owed to a man who for six years shared good fortune and bad, honour and danger, with me. I shan't forget that he left a son. He shall be my son, so soon as I can be a father to him. I am so confused to-day —— "

" Generous man! But do not think so meanly of me. At least accept the money, and let me have an easy conscience."

" What more do you need than my assurance that the money does not belong to me? Or do you want me to rob my friend's fatherless son? for that is what it amounts to. It belongs to him; lay it aside for him."

One notices the lifelike confusion of reasons.

" I understand you. Excuse me if I don't understand exactly how to receive favors. But how did you know that a mother would do more for her son than she would do for her own life?"

No sooner is the door closed upon her than Tellheim says: "Poor, noble woman! I must not forget to destroy the note;" and he takes it from his pocket-book and tears it into fragments. "Who knows," he goes on, "that my misery might not some day lead me to make use of it?" This touch was, and is, most thrilling on the stage.

The next scene, in which Just brings in his bill, showing that he owes his master 91 thalers, 16 groschen, 3 pfennigs, is excellent reading. "Fellow, you are crazy!" says Tellheim. "What are you looking at me for? You don't owe me anything, and I will recommend you to some one of my friends where you will be better off than you can be with me."

"I don't owe you anything, and yet you want to turn me away?"

"Because I am not willing to get into debt to you."

Then Just, who bears a close family likeness to Trim, in Sterne's "Tristram Shandy," recounts his experience with a poodle: "Last winter I was walking by the canal, when I heard a sort of whimpering. I climbed down in the direction of the voice; I thought I was saving a child from drowning, and drew a poodle out of the water. 'All right,' thought I. The poodle followed me; but I'm no great friend of poodles. I tried to get rid of him, but in vain. I whipped him off, but in vain. I would not let him sleep in my room; he lay just outside of the door. If he came near me, I kicked him off; he would howl, look at me, and wag his tail. I have never given him a crumb of bread, and yet I am the only person whose voice he will hear. He leaps about me, and is always showing off his little tricks. He is an ugly cur, but a good dog after all. If he goes on, I shall get fond of poodles." And when Tellheim says that he means to leave the inn, he bids Just to pack up all his things, the pistols that hang at the head of his bed, and, "One thing more: bring the poodle along; do you understand, Just?"

These selections, however, do the play injustice, because they make it appear as if Tellheim were always posing for the proud man; but in fact these characterizations are kept subordinate to the movement of the play. When Minna is chatting with her maid, for instance, we find equal skill. Thus Franziska says: "People seldom speak of the virtue they have, but so much the oftener of the one they lack."

"Do you see, Franziska, you have made a very wise remark?"

"Made? Does one make what just happens to occur to one?"

"And do you know why I like it so much? It applies to my Tellheim."

"And what in the world would you not apply to him?"

"Friends and foes agree that he is the

bravest man in the world. But who ever heard him talk about bravery? He has the most upright heart in the world, but uprightness and generosity are words that never crossed his lips."

"What sort of virtues does he talk about, then?"

"About none, for he has them all."

"I wanted to hear that."

"But wait a minute, let me think. He does talk a good deal about economy. I will say in confidence that I think the man is extravagant."

"Oh yes. I have often heard him mention truth and constancy to you; how if he should happen to be a flirt?"

Lessing could be light as well as pathetic. One last extract shall show this rarer quality of feeling. Werner tries to force some money on him, which Tellheim refuses. "It is not proper that I should be your debtor."

"Not proper? When that hot day, which the sun and the enemy both made hot, and your groom had gone astray with the canteen, and you came to me and said ' Werner, have you got anything to drink?' and I held out mine to you, did n't you take it and drink from it? Was that proper? By my poor soul, as if a drink of wretched water at that moment was not more than all that stuff! (he holds out the purse.) Take it, dear Major! Just imagine it's water. God created it for us all."

" You agonize me; don't you understand that I don't want to be your debtor?"

"Oh! that's very different. You don't want to be my debtor? But how if you happened to be already? Or don't you owe anything to the man who caught the blow that was aimed at your head, and another time cut off the arm that was about to send a bullet into you? How could you owe this man any more? Or is my neck less important than my purse? If that is a proper thought, by my poor soul, it's in abominably poor taste." And when Tellheim still refuses,

Werner fires this parting shot: "I have often thought: How will it be when you are old and crippled; when you have nothing left; when you must beg your way from door to door? Then I thought: No, you won't have to beg; there 's Major Tellheim, you 'll go to him, he will share his last penny with you, he will support you as long as you live, and you 'll die an honest man. I don't think so any longer. Whoever won't take anything from me when he needs it and I 've got it, won't give me anything when he has it and I need it. Oh, very well!" The reader will notice the foreboding of the tactics which Minna employed.

Yet there is one thing to be noticed in these scenes, and this is the way in which Lessing addresses the sensibility of his hearers. At a time when Klopstock, and the translations from the English were moistening every eye, he drew this reserved officer and the intelligent heroine in a manner that was as far as possible removed from the effusive. In one place where they are talking, she says: "Patience, you still love me! that is enough for me. But what a tone I 've fallen into! An odious, melancholy, contagious tone. I must resume a natural one. Now, my poor dear fellow, you still love me, you have your Minna, and are unhappy? Just hear what a poor conceited creature your Minna was — is. She fancied, she fancies that she is your only happiness. Come, out with all your unhappiness! She wishes to see how much she outweighs it. —Well?"

"I am not used to complaining."

"That is right. Next to bragging, I don't know what is more detestable in a soldier than complaining. But there is a certain cold, indifferent way of speaking of one's bravery and misfortunes."

"Which is yet bragging and complaining all the same," rejoins Tellheim.

Does not this scene fairly represent Lessing's views of the new sensibility? While

his contemporaries manufactured pathos, he
sang the beauty of reserve with the same
reasonable intelligence that he showed in
contrasting the Prussian and the Saxon, and
in pointing out the reconciliation between
them when German patriotism was revelling
in the celebration of Hermann and other
remote heroes. The new Romanticism did
not address him; he had the love of com-
pleteness, of perfect form, which distin-
guished the generation before the romantic
authors began to write; he was the last
of a long line; they were the crude
beginners of a new epoch. His main task
was correcting and classifying the past.
Thereby he, to be sure, made the way
smoother for his successors because the
work of every generation is built up on
what went before it, but the confusion of
the new men only disturbed him. Like
Klopstock, he disliked Goethe's "Werther,"
which was the declaration of war for a later
generation. Whereas they were turbid and

uncertain, he who had won for himself the command of what seemed best in the world could not endure the inevitable abandonment of old models just as soon as these had been cleared of the dust of centuries. In his eyes the new men were going hopelessly astray. He had restored antiquity to its proper place, he had helped to bring Shakespeare into repute, he had overthrown Gottsched and proved the unwisdom of the vague Swiss critics, but in stating the laws of tragedy as Aristotle meant them instead of as the French imitators of Seneca had perverted them, he had left it to Herder to show how much beauty there was outside of the classics. He was the greatest of the æsthetic critics, while Herder established historical criticism which is now trying to get a foothold in English-speaking nations, and has placed Germany at the head of the world in most matters of study. The manner in which Lessing turned his back on the modern excessive sensibility is illustrative of his whole position with regard to the new movement, and a most striking proof of the comparative unfruitfulness of mere æsthetic criticism. So far as æsthetic beauty is concerned, no comparison is possible between Lessing's dignified, impressive handling of the emotions and the wallowing, gushing enthusiasm of which we have seen traces in Klopstock and some of his admirers; yet their very excesses held latent the seeds of much that has enriched the world as the eighteenth century at its best could never have done. The future lay in those absurdities, to which Lessing's back was turned while he rediscovered the golden past. We can see in the history of English literature the same truth, that in the blunders made by the fervours of inexperience, there is a new revelation seeking expression, just as in the tiresome high spirits and chronic bubbling disobedience of a child there may lie a finer, more original character than in the smug docility of the precocious prig. Let us not forget that the only consolation of the German generals whom Napoleon was forever thrashing, was that they had at any rate fought according to the rules.

If, in comparing English with German literature, we go back to Goldsmith, it is easy to see how superior his smooth and discreetly tender verse must have seemed to those who were bidden to admire Wordsworth's occasionally hoarse and frequently tedious descriptions of nature, but in Wordsworth there was a new view of the world laid open to readers and thinkers. Perfection of work is an indication of approaching change, but it is rare for the man who has been brought up on the complete form to be able to admire the following one. Yet every labourer at the task of building up civilization even unconsciously raises the edifice higher, although each one carries his own hod and is apt to grumble at his fellow-workers. The very qualities that enable a man to do one sort of work tend to dull his appreciation and comprehension of another.

Moreover, there is in literature a quickly vanishing moment of perfection, as there is one of legality in the course of a revolution, which is speedily lost sight of in the whirl of change. The revolution may have every right on its side, but it demands for its accomplishment that all the previous laws be broken before a healthier society can be organized; yet there is an inevitable division at this point between those who are bound by feeling, habit, and education to uphold existing laws, and those who look beyond the laws to the grander final result. In our own history, and notably in the scruples of those who wondered whether the government was justified in calling for troops at the beginning of our war, we may see an example of the latter class. In literature, Lessing belonged to the other men, who hold to legality; whose work is far removed from the anarchy of the revolutionists, and who prefer perfecting the past to making rash experiments with the future. Whereas his contemporaries busied themselves with the extravagant representation of the middle ages and the unrestrained emotions of their own day, he at one time wrote imitations of Greek plays and never followed their laxer course.

The "Emilia Galotti," too, is full of the eighteenth-century impulse, although that quality is far from being the most noticeable thing about the play. It is the fruit of long study of the drama and its laws, for against Lessing there cannot be brought the current and very old accusation that a critic is one who has failed in creative work; on the contrary, he was a critic whose lessons were full of profit, and who, after stirring up a hornet's nest, brought out some original work as a model for those whom his criticism had offended. His "Minna" was a model comedy; there yet remained the tra-

gedy to be done. In the interval between
the two plays he had written his " Hamburger Dramaturgie," in which he had discussed the laws and the best conditions of the
drama with a vividness, an impressiveness,
and a fund of learning that one is not accustomed to associate with a theatrical critic.
All this consideration of Aristotle, of Corneille, of Voltaire, of Shakespeare, bore rich
fruit, although his appreciation of the great
English tragedian was very different from
the unbounded admiration that the younger
men felt for him. As early as 1759, in one
of his *Literaturbriefe*, while reproving Gottsched for copying the French stage, he
said that if the early critic had translated
some of Shakespeare's masterpieces with a
few slight alterations,[1] he would have done

---

[1] Cholevius, "Geschichte der deutschen Poesie," theil i.,
p. 537, has some interesting remarks on this matter, pointing out how impossible it would have been for Gottsched to
do what Lessing wished that he had done. As we have seen,
the poor man had no choice, and Lessing's error may serve
as a warning against neglecting the historical conditions.
It is not unlike regretting that the Greeks did not use modern artillery in the siege of Troy.

better than he did in making the Germans acquainted with Corneille and Racine; that Shakespeare would have inspired writers, for a genius can be kindled only by a genius, and most easily by one who owes all his merit to nature, and does not repel admirers by the tedious perfections of art. But, while here Lessing mentions Shakespeare's apparent lack of art, he goes on to point out that, even with regard to art, Shakespeare is a much greater tragic poet than Corneille.

Nearly ten years later, when Wieland's translation and Gerstenberg's commentary had appeared, he spoke of Shakespeare in the "Hamburger Dramaturgie;" but although he was then writing his "Emilia Galotti," he found no inspiration in Shakespeare. But in a later period, between 1773 and 1787, we see the influence of Shakespeare dominant in the work of the younger men. Lessing's root lay in the classic literature. His thorough study of the earlier masters naturally turned him away from the crude domestic tragedy which had inspired "Miss Sara Sampson," while at the same time it taught him to avoid the error of the French classical drama in unnecessarily narrowing the limits that were imposed by the critics under the shadow of Aristotle's name. On the one hand, it taught him the folly of a colourless copy of the French plays,—his last words in the "Dramaturgie" had been that, without being a poet, there was not one of Corneille's plays which he could not improve, — and, on the other, he had learned not to mistake a mere sentimental attack on the feelings for real tragic action. In the tragedy that was growing up since Lillo's famous—rather than great—play, the new notion of the importance of the individual, which had been lost sight of in the prominence given to cultivation and to social position, was beginning to assert itself anew by means of the sympathy that was felt for a man who suffered, even if his suf-

ferings were, so to speak, the mere result of
accident, and not of serious tragic fault.
The main point was that the individual suffered; the cause of his misery was unim-
portant.   But in Lessing's eyes the immu-
table laws of art admitted no such limitation.
He determined to write a tragedy in which
the final issue should be the natural result
of the action of the characters, and not a
mere external, cruel accident.   The result
was " Emilia Galotti."

It is interesting to notice that the under-
lying plot was taken from the old Roman
story of Virginia, wherein Lessing showed
his willingness to meet the classical drama-
tists on their own ground; but in adapting
the plot to modern times he showed them in
what way the ancients should be held as
models, while he was able to make clear to
his contemporaries how the present was to
be treated.   That he deliberately chose that
story with this conscious purpose cannot be
directly affirmed, but his selection had at

any rate this double advantage. Yet the
story of "Emilia Galotti" is not to be compared, line for line, with the classic original.
He made no copy on tracing-paper; the
whole notion of peril for the state, that
counts for much in the Roman original,
disappears from his play; all that is left is
the tragic story of the young girl's honour
preserved by death.

Every one who knows anything about
German literature is familiar with this play
and will recall its incidents. Emilia is
about to be married to the Count Appiani,
and the young Prince who has already seen
her and fallen in love with her is beside
himself on hearing this fact. His minister
and intimate adviser, Marinelli, begs him to
entrust the matter to him. The Prince ac-
cedes, and Marinelli arranges the assassina-
tion of the Count, and the abduction of Emilia with her mother. A mask of politeness
hides their real intentions. The pretext
that the murder of the Count demands a

judicial investigation is made the reason for detaining the two women, but the father is admitted to see them. Emilia acknowledges the peril of her position. This it is that induces the father to kill her, a deed for which she thanks him as she dies.

It is not new for this termination of the play to call forth wonder. At the time of its first appearance numerous critics pointed out the unsatisfactory end. Goethe, indeed, suggested that Emilia was conscious of feeling an interest in the Prince, but there is every reason to doubt whether Lessing could have permitted himself to represent this accidental emotion, and one, too, that is nowhere stated or implied as the turning-point of a tragedy in which clearness was as essential as truth. The hypothesis is one that could explain better the plays written after Lessing, when sudden passions took the place that had in earlier times been occupied by equally mysterious fate. That Emilia Galotti, whose betrothed had just been slain, could contemplate for a moment the probable fascinations of the vicious society at the house of Marinelli, is something simply surprising, and it may be fair to adopt for explanation the hypothesis that, in Emilia, Lessing tried to draw a woman who should represent an old-fashioned ideal of domesticity and maidenly reserve. In a letter to his brother he wrote: "Girlish heroines and philosophers are not at all to my taste. I know in unmarried girls no higher virtues than piety and obedience;" of independence he has nothing to say, and by thus depriving Emilia of those qualities that assure safety in the circumstances wherein she finds herself, he has no other way of cutting the web that has formed about her than by putting her to death. Thus villainy is baffled, and an impossible, or at least an antiquated, ideal is preserved. Yet the new men, with one consent, criticised this solution. Lessing here, as elsewhere, clung to the past, and, with every qualification in his possession, he left the future of the German stage in the hands of men who, however crudely, let women count as characters, not as mere accumulations of domestic virtues.

Yet it is impossible to speak too highly of the mechanical execution of the play; this quality alone sufficed to make it a model for future workers, and its influence is easily detected in Schiller's "Kabale and Liebe." This latter play is a direct attact on the viciousness of German princelings, and it is easy to suppose that the keen intelligence of Lessing did not fail to understand the truth which was very obvious to those who saw the play, that the condemnation of licentious rulers was capable of very vivid application in Germany. Goethe, in one of his talks with Eckermann (Feb. 7, 1827), lamented the polemical tone in Lessing's work, ascribing its existence to the wretchedness of the times in which he lived. He said, "In the 'Emilia Galotti,' he gave vent

to his grudge against the princes; in 'Nathan,' his grudge against the priests." Yet
if this was true—and there seems no good
ground for doubting it, for Lessing had
never been spoiled by courts—his spirit
was rather a correcting one than it was an
iconoclastic wrath, such as that which animated Schiller. He had as little of the
revolutionary spirit in political as in literary
matters; the solution of the difficulties that
beset that period was like the one that we
are all striving to find now: it was to set
right existing evils, not to rise and over-
throw them violently. This destructive
feeling belonged only to the younger men,
and was gradually lifting its head in letters
just as now the spirit of revolution that
manifests itself in fierce detestation of government appears in literature as a desire to
paint the ordinary man as he is, not as people imagine that others think that he is.

In the "Nathan the Wise," again, Lessing sought a similar solution; the whole

play is, as it were, an apologue illustrative
of the views he held about religious questions. One of the most widespread of the
movements that marked the period of enlightenment was the excitement in behalf
of free-thinking, that, like much else of the
best inspiration of the last century, had its
origin in England. It was one chapter of
the great lesson of freedom that demanded
release from the shackles of authority in
politics, literature, and ecclesiasticism, and of
all these subjects the relation of man to the
church is not the least important. Yet, inasmuch as the tendency of the church manifested itself mainly in a desire to subordinate
society to its control, wherein it should hold
a position of chief magistrate, the opposition
limited itself mainly to opposing the claims
of priestcraft. This must be continually
borne in mind, if we are anxious to form a
just conception of the controversy. It was
not a magnificent, inspiring religion that
was attacked, but a petrified, heartless social

form, in which a feeling of simple devotion would have been as out of place as one of Goethe's lyrics in a tragedy of Gottsched's. It was universally agreed that it was not religion in itself that was assaulted, any more than literature was the object of those who denounced the rules. Questions are not answered until they are asked; and not yet was the discussion begun as to whether or not some form of religion was necessary. The antagonists of a corrupt religion were Deists; of the later religious excitement of the Methodists, Atheists. In England the fight was always on the outskirts; there was no attack on the citadel. The Deists, by their very name, showed that they acknowledged a purer and simpler form of belief, which they would fain establish. The *Infâme* against which Voltaire raged was not the religious sense, but a corrupt religion; one marked in France by every vice of persecution and intolerance that inspired his hate. In England, religion is always a

very important part of the social structure.
Swedenborg noticed that in heaven the
English kept very much to themselves, and
free-thought has been doubly dangerous in
that country, because it has been unfashion-
able. The avowed non-believer has been a
social outcast. In France, however, non-
belief was a more serious matter, and threatened its supporters with more serious trou-
bles than was the case across the channel ;
so that whatever one may think of Voltaire's
religious sentiments, it is impossible not to
admire his noble defence, in the face of real
danger, of the victims of religious persecution. In Germany the questions concerned
were much less important; yet even here, in
the home of modern theology, they excited
an interest which they lacked in England.
There was no such contrast as in France between the lives and the duties of the eccles-
iastics; the higher officials of the church
were not leaders in debauchery, as was
sometimes the case in the neighbouring

country, and persecution did not go so far as to burn its victims at the stake. Yet an arid, hide-bound orthodoxy existed, against which Lessing fought for some time, and it was this contest that called forth the "Nathan." This play, then, held the same position in regard to his theological discussions that his "Emilia" did to his "Dramaturgie;" it was the creative equivalent of his critical work. It inculcated the same lesson of tolerance that was the aim of the whole movement. Whereas in France the strife was complicated by the way in which Voltaire felt compelled to mine the ground beneath his dangerous opponents, by disproving the basis of revealed religion, here the contest took place in a field where intellectual controversy had more weight. The question was one that excited general interest, while in England the common feeling had been one of indignation against the men who insisted on brawling instead of letting things run on in the old-fashioned way. Having started the question, tho English did not care for an answer. It lost practical importance for them, and, as they often did with exciting theories, they, as it were, transported the serious consideration of it to other countries, as if it were a convict. English literature resumed its glib acceptance of all the social conditions of life as if no harassing questions existed to torment the anxious, just as now it runs on as if vice and black error did not exist in the world. Nothing can better illustrate the difference between England and Germany at this period than the contemplation of the impossibility that a play like Lessing's "Nathan" should have appeared in London. The stage was devoted to such new plays as Foote's farces, the comedies of Sheridan and Goldsmith, and Home's tragedies, which had equally little to do with serious thought. Germany, however, was busy with the examination of the many new notions that were in the air, and was preparing for the prominent place it was about to take in the romantic revival. As in France, the men who were making over literature were also making over the thought of many men on other subjects; and the point that was reached by Lessing here bore strong resemblance, in its wisdom and reasonableness, to what Lessing had striven to attain in his purely literary work. Toleration is in no way a revolutionary step; it implies, too, the same acceptance of the past, but of a past shorn of its growth of bigotry, that we have seen in Lessing's elevation of the stage. Orthodoxy had become a thing of hard and fast rule like the pseudo-classical tragedy, and in his treatment of both we may see Lessing's desire to bring forward saner notions, but by way of modification, not of revolution.

It is with truth that the "Nathan" is called the one play which is full of the eighteenth century spirit;[1] all that is best

[1] See Mr. John Morley's "Diderot," p. 227.

in that interesting period finds expression
there; the ideal was a high one: toleration,
reasonable endurance of others. What can
be grander than such a lesson? But its
very perfection prophesied its brief existence. It was an ideal attained by a few,
but too remote from the popular comprehension to endure. It lacked a sufficient
historical basis. Tolerance is only really
learned otherwise than by reason, and this
elevated point was a quickly vanishing one,
which was soon lost sight of. It was, like
all the eighteenth century thought, an
essentially aristocratic position, the doctrine of the remnant, and as unable to save
the world as a few champions are to settle
a modern war by single combat.

No; at the very moment when tragedy
was made simple, direct, and clear, it slipped
into confusion and became the outlet for
hitherto unknown emotions in the hands of
Schiller and Goethe; and, as soon as religious toleration was acquired, the new virtue

had to be kept in busy practice to keep the peace now seriously threatened by the new forms of evangelicalism, mediæval Catholicism, and absolute infidelity. The point that Lessing had reached still remained to be reached again by the larger multitude without; and during all the subsequent confusion and reaction the eighteenth century perfection of form and clear intelligence have had their influence in showing what has to be attained by the orderly arrangement of our more motley knowledge. For with this last century has come the deluge of new thoughts, forgotten emotions, the reviving memory of the past, and, supervising all, the historical sense which demanded their intelligent arrangement. And along with the scientific enlargement of this century, of which those who do not comprehend the physiology of a common pump are forever boasting, is the emotional one, the importance whereof can be hardly overestimated. The two are blended, for example, in our dissatisfaction with the vague historical setting of the eighteenth century tragedies. "Nathan the Wise," like all the rest, has its scene laid in a dim region, one that lies to the eastward, we may say, rather than that it is in the East, and this remoteness from historical or geographical exactness well represents the abstract intellectual unity of the whole play. It was the geometry of intellectual discussion which our grandfathers studied,— some of our later methods may remind us of the sports of the kindergarten, — and in the absence of local colour we see the absence of many of the conflicting difficulties that embarrass these questions for us. This, at least, may be said, that in the diagrams which expressed their lucid thought there is conveyed an eternal truth which humanity must learn in its own way, by experience. The remnant cannot save our souls, we must save them ourselves, and their remote enunciation of the truth is the statement of a proposition which we must solve out of our own lives. That our answer will rest on the same basis as that of Lessing cannot be affirmed any more than it can be certain that our best tragedies will be based on Aristotle's rules; but, whatever the future may have in store for us, the toleration which Lessing saw will render us able to respect even an unfamiliar way of regarding this momentous question.

"Nathan the Wise" is scarcely a play; Lessing himself called it rather a dramatic poem, which exactly defines it, although it is still acted in the German theatres with commendable piety. The core of the play or poem lies in the parable of the rings which Nathan recounts to Saladin, who, it may be fair to presume, is the ideal monarch with a predisposition to consulting philosophers on religion, as the crowned heads of the last century, Frederick the Great and Catharine of Russia, consulted them on questions of literature and heard them on government, besides following them in all

their many investigations. The story was
an old one, but it receives a new form in
Lessing's hands. The Sultan asks Nathan
what in his opinion is the true religion, and
Nathan answers with the parable of a man
in the East who owned a ring of inestimable
value, which possessed the secret power of
endearing to God and man the wearer who
believed in its magic quality. He bequeathed it to the dearest of his sons, who
in turn should leave it to his dearest son,
and so on; the owner, it was said, by virtue
of this ring, should be the head of the family. Finally, the ring came into the possession of the father of three sons, who, being
unable to decide among them, had two imitations made so exactly alike that he himself could not distinguish them, and these
he gave to his sons on his death-bed.
Thereupon arose strife as to which was the
head of the family. Each one felt sure
that his father had not deceived him and
was ready to accuse his brother of dishon-

esty. They appealed to a judge, whose decision ran thus, that, inasmuch as the ring possessed the magic quality of making its wearer loved, he need only find which of the brothers filled that condition. "What, none? Then you are all deceived deceivers. All the rings are false. Probably the true ring was lost. But I advise each of you to imagine his ring to be the true one, and to go away; then let each one strive to show this power in his own ring.

"Let him aid this power with humility, with earnest tolerance and kindness, with sincere devotion," and in time, after thousands of thousands of years, a wiser judge may give the exact answer. In other words, righteousness and devotion may alone solve the question.

If this play is read simultaneously with Lessing's prose writings on religion, it will be seen that according to our modern notions, he would be classified among or very near the orthodox, yet in his own day he was detested by the class that in a hundred years has learned to enlarge its boundaries. By some common people his death, which soon followed, was supposed to be a special act of the devil, who spirited him away miraculously; others maintained that the physicians, from a sense of high duty, refused to cure him when he was ill; but the more intelligent naturally mourned his untimely loss. They recognized the value of his lesson, and, to speak of the " Nathan " alone, we may easily see that if toleration is advisable among Christians, Jews, and Mohammedans, it is no less desirable for atheists and pagans as well. The seeds of thought, *fermenta cogitationis*, which Lessing boasted that he planted, are true in the larger field because they are true in the narrower one which he knew. This stimulation of thought was his greatest work; and since that task is, from its nature, fragmentary and never to be completed, there is a certain roundness at least in the choice of subjects which he treated. It did not fall to his lot to take part in the great enlargement of men's interests which was the work of the romantic school. That was accomplished by a new generation which was already growing up around him.

The distinction between the eighteenth century and the present one is clearly manifested in a remark of Lessing, which has met with nothing but unqualified approval: "Not the truth of which anyone is, or supposes himself to be, possessed, but the upright endeavour he has made to aim at truth, makes the worth of the man. For not by the possession, but by the investigation, of truth, are his powers expanded, wherein alone his growing perfection consists. Possession makes us easy, indolent, proud. If God held all truth shut in his right hand, and in his left nothing but the ever restless instinct for truth, though with the condition of for ever and ever erring, and should say to me, 'Choose!' I should humbly bow to his left hand, and say, 'Father, give! pure truth is for thee alone.'" This eloquent utterance, however, with its left-handed compliment to truth, — as if truth were an answer to a puzzle, and not the only thing that makes life valuable, — is full of the same eighteenth century wisdom that characterizes the remarks of those men of the present day who regard education as something that does good, not by itself, but by "exercising the mind." Fontenelle had already said: "Si j'avais la main remplie de vérités, je me garderais bien de l'ouvrir," so that Lessing is relieved of some of the opprobrium that might be hastily accorded him. But, idling aside, may we not see in the latter half of this statement not only the notion which Goethe inherited and in turn bequeathed to some conservatives of the present day, that this world is created for the intellectual delight of a few educated people, but also that feeling of dependence on the past which began to crumble at the end of the eighteenth century? The destruction of the Bastille was but an outward and visible sign of the breaking loose of modern men from authority. The iron chains then broken were not the only fetters snapped; indeed, modern scholarship may be said to date from Wolf's "Prolegomena" (1795), and modern scholarship has destroyed many bugbears. It may be affirmed of the "Prolegomena" that they marked the period when modern men had matured sufficiently to look the classics in the face. The book appeared not long before Wordsworth and Coleridge began to found the new poetry in England, and at the very time when real literature began to exist in Germany. The past had done its best work in educating men who spoke, not merely to the present, but to the future — the only grateful audience. The man who at this present day should refuse to grasp the truth, in order that he might exercise his mind in searching for it, would not be loved. The opinion has arisen that the truth is perhaps as valuable as any one man's symmetrical development; for this, after all, might be attained by exercising in a wholly profitless way, and, moreover, no man will work to bring out a muscle as he will to save his life.

Yet, as nothing starts in a complete form in this world, we may see in some of Lessing's last writings the forebodings of the altered notions that were to inspire the younger men. In his "Erziehung des Menschengeschlechts" there are distinct statements of the growth in the past, and the probable growth in the future, of humanity. "Why," he asks in the beginning, "why should we not rather, in all positive religions, regard nothing more than the course in which the human understanding of every place alone can develop, and must further develop itself, instead of ridiculing or denouncing it? Nothing else in the world deserves our scorn or wrath, should religion alone deserve them? Is it

possible that God should have his hand in
everything, but not in our errors?" Then
follow the detached thoughts that make up
the memorable treatise, wherein he traced
briefly the growth of humanity: —

What education is to the single individual, revelation is to the whole human race.

Education is revelation coming to the individual,
and revelation is education coming to the race.

.   .   .   .   .   .

Education gives the individual nothing that he had
not in himself, and so of revelation, it gives humanity
nothing to which reason could not attain by its own
unaided resources.

Then he goes on to say that time may
bring to the world a new revelation which
shall be to Christianity what Christianity
itself was to what went before it, when man
will do right because it is right, not because
it ensures certain rewards.

There is no need of pointing out Lessing's
fine moral enthusiasm; what concerns us
here is the declaration of a possible and
probable development of humanity in the
future. No longer did he look back with

regret to a golden past; the present was full of promise, and there is here dimly stated what was to be announced more clearly by Herder, that the condition of man is one of growth. Just before the great dramatic revolution broke out, Lessing died. He had already expressed dissatisfaction with Goethe's "Götz," which indicated no respect for Aristotle, and for the "Werther," wherein was announced the new truth that reason alone cannot move the world; that for this is required the combination of qualities that go to make up every human being.[1] Reason alone is as inefficient to make a thorough person as is muscular strength alone to make a man healthy. Everything that man undertakes to produce, whether by action, word, or in whatsoever way, ought to spring from the union of all his faculties. "All that is iso-

---

[1] In Lessing's comments on the novel, he said: "Do you imagine that a Roman or Greek youth would have taken his life in this fashion and for this reason?" To Goethe this was an argument as remote as the Greek oracles.

lated is contemptible," is Goethe's statement of Hamann's and Herder's teachings. It was this widening of the influences that the new time had to establish, and in parting with Lessing we have behind us the man who, in his dealings with reason alone, showed how the new lesson had to be taught, — by theory and practice, by sincerity and direct study, by patience and toleration. The high mark that he had reached with his principles had to be attained anew with the new principles.

This may be a fitting place to close. We have traced roughly the slow degrees by which Germany passed through its period of apprenticeship. Everywhere, in form at least, it kept step with the movements of thought that held sway over all of Europe, from Portugal to Norway; for modern literature is essentially a .unit; what happened in one country repeated itself in the main in every other, just as the vicissitudes of growth are repeated in every human being between his birth and maturity, with differences, to be sure, in each case, depending on the personal characteristics. Yet these characteristics cannot be properly understood until it is discovered how much the various phenomena that we observe in the individual are part of the common experience of the race. When this is done, it becomes easier to study intelligently what is left. And there is certainly enough left to reward the student. Especially in the history of romanticism in Germany does the peculiar quality of the Germans assert itself. As the pseudo-classicism made its headquarters in France, where it found a congenial home, so the romantic spirit was more momentous in Germany than elsewhere, and found in Goethe a fuller expression than in any other one man. Perhaps at some future time we may study the form that romanticism took in that land, when we may see how the confusion of its history shut it off from that return to its

own past which was an important part of
the romantic revival in England, and how
the development of the qualities that we
have so far seen only in their crudity gave
Germany its prominence in intellectual
matters.